# What Others Are Saying About
## *The Three Princes*

Every book Tom Julien has written has always touched me. I have often referred to them and benefited immensely from them. The author has vividly and convincingly portrayed the world of three beings, Adam, Satan, and Christ, overarching from one end of eternity to the other. This is an overview of *real* human history, which has been commonly overlooked, resulting in the great loss of spiritual realities. With this book thoughtful readers will be awakened and restored to the reality of the spirit world, which is so commonly ignored in the lives of many people in spite of the fact that the unseen world is more real than the visible world. *The Three Princes* will open the eyes of spiritually slumbering souls and cause them to rise above the one-dimensional world, comprehending the spiritual realities and the road map of our spiritual journey. The readers will gain the hope of glory through the victorious third prince, our Lord Jesus Christ. This book is so revealing and so encouraging.

> **Dr. Sang-Bok David Kim**, *World Evangelical Alliance Chairman, Chancellor of Torch Trinity Graduate School of Theology, Korea*

The Bible is prolific in alerting us to be vigilant regarding our adversary, the devil; yet there is a prevalent tendency to ignore these warnings. The result is a defeated Christian life and a church that is powerless and diverted from God's mission in the world. In this book by Tom Julien the reader will find a comprehensive biblical panorama of this biblical conflict and discover that the victory over our subtle and devious enemy has been procured by the Lamb of God. *The Three Princes* will not only provide valuable insights and understanding, but encouragement to claim that victory and walk in it.

> **Dr. Jerry Rankin**, *President Emeritus, International Mission Board, Southern Baptist Convention*

Tom Julien has done the church a great service in writing *The Three Princes*. Beginning with the conflict between the serpent and Adam in the Garden, he traces the development of that conflict through the end times depicted in The Revelation. In a very readable, balanced manner, Julien provides the needed spiritual-conflict dimension to the worldview that is essential for the understanding of both the Old and the New Testaments. It is required reading for anyone who is serious about personal spiritual growth and effective ministry to others.

**DR. TIMOTHY WARNER**, *former President of Fort Wayne Bible College and Professor at Trinity Evangelical Divinity School*

I vividly remember the ambiance of our New Age home. Coming home from school, I was welcomed by a huge Buddha dominating the living room, incense rising in front of it, windows decorated with Hindu motifs. My father was a Master in an esoteric movement, and I thrived in a worldview defined by energy, reincarnation, and self-hypnosis. Little did I know about the nature of that "other world," which revealed its face when God's grace invaded my life. After the joyful discovery of the Gospel, I was plagued with bizarre, blasphemous thoughts and voices—how could that happen, now that I knew the God of the universe? I am thankful for Tom Julien, whose piety and heart for world vision I greatly admire. His book crafts vividly the reality of the spiritual fight that surrounds the Christian life, exalting the absolute victory of the Lord Jesus Christ. He portrays the grandiose plan of redemption, a salvation that should more accurately be described as a rescue. It's my hope that, upon reading *The Three Princes*, every believer would joyfully give thanks to the Father, "who has qualified you to share in the inheritance of the saints in light. For He has delivered us from the domain of darkness and transferred us to the kingdom of His beloved Son, in whom we have redemption, the forgiveness of sins" (Colossians 1:12-14, NASB).

> **FLORENT VARAK**, *Pastor in Lyon, France, Adjunct Professor in the Geneva Bible Institute*

*The Three Princes* by my friend and colleague Tom Julien gives us biblical insights into angels and demons that make Dan Brown pale in comparison. This is a window into spiritual realities, which every child of God needs to understand in order to live the freedom that God has procured for us at the Cross through His Son Jesus."

> **DR. WALT STUART**, *Pastor and Professor in Pastoral Counseling, Lautenbach, France*

# *the* THREE PRINCES

# *the* THREE PRINCES

## Lifting *the* Veil *on the* Unseen World

### TOM JULIEN

BMH Books
*bmhbooks.com*
P.O. Box 544
Winona Lake, IN 46590

*The Three Princes: Lifting the Veil on the Unseen World*
Copyright ©2011 by Tom Julien

ISBN: 978-0-88469-278-2
RELIGION / Christian Life / Spiritual Warfare

Printed in the United States of America

Published by BMH Books
BMH Books, P.O. Box 544, Winona Lake, IN 46590 USA
*bmhbooks.com*

*To Doris, my beloved wife*
*and teammate for 56 years,*
*absent from the body,*
*but present with the Lord.*

# Table of Contents

# About This Book

THROUGHOUT HISTORY, THREE PRINCES HAVE EXERCISED authority over the earth. The rule of the first, Adam, was pitifully short. His authority was stolen by Satan, the second prince, who brought unspeakable suffering to mankind. This began the supreme drama of all time, the drama of redemption. It is a drama that finds its climax in Satan's defeat and the triumph of the third Prince, Jesus Christ, who became a man in order to win back what the first man had lost. To grasp the magnitude of this drama, in which each of us is playing a significant role, we must lift the veil of the visible and peer into the mysteries of the unseen world.

This book has three purposes. First, it is meant to provide a biblical *worldview* leading to a more complete understanding of God's revelation concerning the rebellion of Satan and the triumph of our Lord in gaining back what Adam lost. The book is written for those who are trying to connect the dots in their grasp of the realities of the unseen world. Hopefully, the reader will be filled with a new sense of awe through a deeper understanding of the glory of God's eternal plan.

Second, it is meant to instill a conscious and ongoing *awareness* of the reality of the unseen world. It is possible to have a theology of the spirit world without a personal consciousness of its existence. Though we are not to become preoccupied with the existence of spirit beings around us, neither are we to ignore their existence.

Too many people have allowed themselves to become prisoners of a one-dimensional view of reality. My prayer is that the scales will fall from their eyes. Some of them are facing continual defeat in their relationship with the Lord because they do not realize that the enemy has established strongholds in their minds and that the "weapons of the world" (2 Corinthians 10:4) are powerless to deliver them from spiritual bondage.

And third, this book is meant to instill in the reader an enduring attitude of *worship* for the Prince who is destined to reign forever. I pray that as you are drawn into the wonder of this unfolding drama of man's redemption, you will fall on your knees in praise and adoration before the Lamb who was slain and who is worthy "to receive power and wealth and wisdom and strength and honor and glory and praise" (Revelation 5:12).

This book is for all who take the Bible seriously, and especially for those who are actively ministering to others. It is my hope that these readers will use this information to provide some theological underpinnings in their ministry toward those who are in need of spiritual freedom. This is not a manual for spiritual warfare; it is meant to provide a foundational base. Many excellent tools are available to those who are helping free people from their bondage, such as Neil Anderson's *Steps to Freedom in Christ*. Hopefully the following pages will lead to a more adequate comprehension of the truths underlying these tools.

Though many have encouraged me to put this material into book form, I owe special gratitude to my coworker Jay Bell for his persistence. For Jay the concepts in this book are not abstract truths; he and his wife Jan effectively apply them in their widespread counseling ministry, which has brought freedom to a large number of believers who have suffered spiritual bondage. The pastoral team of my church has given invaluable input in our weekly discussions of these chapters. I am greatly indebted to Terry White and Kelsey Mitchener of BMH Books, as well as Jesse Deloe, for their excellent editorial work, and to my son Terry for the cover design.

Read these pages as you would read a drama. Plunge your mind deeply into God's revelation of His great plan; you will gain new insights into truth that may have become commonplace for you. May you begin each day by reaffirming your authority in Christ, seated in Him at the right hand of God. And may you go into your world clothed with His armor, filled with His power, armed with the sword of His Spirit, and permeating your life with prayer.

# Foreword

## Dr. Neil T. Anderson

"A MIGHTY FORTRESS IS OUR GOD, A BULWARK NEVER failing." For centuries Christians have sung this powerful song written by Martin Luther. They may be less familiar with another phrase in this time-tested anthem: "Although this world with devils filled." Some segments of the modern church either diminish or deny the reality of that statement, but it is just as true today as it was then and as it was in the days of Christ. The faithful church has always believed in a personal devil who rules this world with a horde of fallen angels, otherwise known as demons. Jesus referred to Satan as the ruler of this world, and the apostle John wrote that "the whole world lies in the power in the evil one" (1 John 5:19, NASB).

"Do you mean to tell me that there are demons where I live?" I'm sure there are, but there are also germs where you live. If you are looking for germs and fearful of them, you will become a hypochondriac. The proper response is to live a healthy, balanced life. Your immune system will protect you. There are demons in this world! So, live a righteous life. If that be the case, then why do we need to know that there are demons in this world? We need to know that there are demons in the spiritual realm for the same reason we need to know that there are germs in the physical realm.

There was a time, not too long ago, that we didn't know about germs. Consequently, doctors didn't scrub up or sterilize their equipment, and people died. Antibiotics weren't known, and many precautions for cleanliness weren't taken. Now we know better and people are living much longer. If there were no demons to tempt, accuse, and deceive us, then there would be no need to put on the armor of God and take every thought captive to the obedience of Christ (2 Corinthians 10:5).

The apostle Paul wrote, "The Spirit clearly says that in later times some will abandon the faith and follow deceiving spirits and things taught by demons" (1 Timothy 4:1). That is presently happening all over the world. I have personally discipled hundreds of Christians who were hearing "voices" and being harassed by tempting and condemning thoughts. They were not mentally ill. In the vast majority of cases it proved to be a spiritual battle for their minds. The apostle Paul also wrote, "I am afraid that just as Eve was deceived by the serpent's cunning, your minds may somehow be led astray from your sincere and pure devotion to Christ" (2 Corinthians 11:3). One lady wrote:

> For years I had these "voices" in my head. There were four in particular and sometimes what seemed like loud choruses of them. When the subject of schizophrenia would come up on television, I would think to myself, *I know I am not schizophrenic, but what is this in my head?* I was tortured, mocked, and jeered. Every thought I had was second-guessed; consequently I had zero self-esteem. I wished they would be quiet and wondered if other people had this problem as well. When I learned from you about taking every thought captive to the obedience of Christ, I came to recognize them for what they were, and I was able to make them leave. That was an amazing and beautiful thing, to be fully quiet in my mind, after so many years of torment.

Martin Luther's antidote for this spiritual battle was Jesus, that name above all names. Jesus came for three primary reasons (see Colossians 2:13-15). First, to die for our sins, which removes the enmity between us and God. Second, He came to give us life. What Adam and Eve lost in the fall was eternal life, and Jesus came that we might have that life. Third, He came to undo the works of Satan (1

John 3:8). That is just as much a part of the gospel as the ιαι. our sins are forgiven, and this part of the gospel is what much of the world is waiting to hear. The dominant religion in the world is spiritism or animism. Spiritists make offerings to appease the deities, and they consult quack doctors or shamans who try to manipulate the spiritual world. We have the privilege to announce to the world that Satan and his demons are disarmed and that every believer who is alive in Christ has spiritual authority over them.

Paul wrote, "So let us put aside the deeds of darkness and put on the armor of light," and he amplifies on the latter when he admonishes Christians to "Clothe yourselves with the Lord Jesus Christ" (Romans 13:12-14). Putting on the armor of God (Ephesians 6:10-18) is essentially the same as putting on the Lord Jesus Christ. We need to do this, because "our struggle is not against flesh and blood, but against the rulers, against the authorities, against the powers of this dark world and against the spiritual forces of evil in the heavenly realms" (v. 12). The term "heavenly realms" is not referring to some physical location. It refers to the spiritual realm that is all around us. It is hard for Westerners to understand that the spiritual realm is just as real as the physical realm. "So we fix our eyes not on what is seen, but on what is unseen. For what is seen is temporary, but what is unseen is eternal" (2 Corinthians 4:18). There are no physical sanctuaries in this world. Our only sanctuary is our position in Christ.

The High Priestly Prayer in John 17:6-26 reveals the first concern that our Lord has for the church that He was leaving behind to carry on His work. "My prayer is not that you take them out of the world but that you protect them from the evil one. They are not of the world, even as I am not of it. Sanctify them by the Truth; your word is truth" (vv. 15-17). Knowing the truth is our first line of defense. Note that we are not called to dispel the darkness. We are called to turn on the light. We are not told to stop thinking negative thoughts. We are told to think upon that which is true, lovely, and right. Jesus continues by praying that we all be united in Him (vv. 20, 21).

If you wanted to stop God's plans, what would you do? I know what I would do, because I think I know what Satan is doing. First,

I would try to divide your mind, because a double-minded person is unstable in all his ways. Second, I would try to divide your marriage, because a house divided against itself cannot stand. Third, I would try to divide the body of Christ, because united we stand, but divided we fall. If we don't know who our enemy is, we are like blind-folded warriors who strike out at ourselves and each other.

My friend, Tom Julien, has written a powerful book revealing the spiritual nature of this world as seen through the grid of Scripture. There is no way that one can understand the message of the Bible without having a biblical worldview. The Bible clearly reveals the struggle between good and evil, between the false prophets and the true prophets, between the father of lies and the Spirit of Truth, and between the kingdom of darkness and the kingdom of God. This book will give you the divine perspective of all the critical events recorded in Scripture. A casual reading won't do. You must study this text and think through the implications of what it means to be a part of this cosmic battle in which we are all involved.

DR. NEIL T. ANDERSON, *Founder and President Emeritus of Freedom in Christ Ministries*

# Introduction

Go to any library and you will find dozens if not hundreds of books that recount the history of mankind. Some are fascinating; others will bore you with their endless details. They all have one thing in common, however. They are one-dimensional. They tell man's story from a purely human viewpoint.

What if you could go to a library and check out some DVDs that portray the history of mankind in more than one dimension? What if there were some technology that would make the realities of the unseen world just as visible as those of our material world? What if you had eyes to see beyond the veil of the visible to learn what is going on around your life in the world of spirits at this very instant?

The Bible makes it clear that God created a world that is far greater than what we see with our eyes. In Colossians 1:16 we read that the Lord created things both visible and invisible. In the Scriptures these two dimensions are often termed "heavenly" and "earthly." Heaven is not only a domain beyond the clouds; it is also the spiritual dimension of the world in which we live, and it is as real as the visible world. Just as there are formidable obstacles in the visible world, there are obstacles in the invisible world. Just as there is real conflict in the visible world, there is real conflict in the unseen world—conflict which affects you and me.

The fact that our senses are equipped to perceive only the visible world in no way means that the invisible world does not exist. It only proves the inadequacy of our present powers of perception. From the beginning to the end of the Bible, God lifts the veil that separates us from the invisible world, revealing the activity of spirit beings. These spirit beings are not the souls of departed humans, as people of many cultures believe. They are beings created by God to be His messengers.

Seeing life with a purely secular worldview is like looking at a 3-D movie without the special glasses. If you use the Bible as the tool by which you view reality, you will begin a journey that will lift the curtain on the most overwhelming and breathtaking drama ever played out throughout eternity. At its core are the most vigilantly guarded secrets of all times.

If you are not accustomed to thinking in this way, the things you have just read might seem strange, or even scary. In our Western worldview, whatever does not fit into our rational way of thinking is usually reserved for science fiction or superstition. Although the overwhelming majority of non-Western people have no doubts about the existence of the spirit world, we Westerners have been educated to accept only what we can see as far as everyday life is concerned.

Some years ago I was leading a Bible study at a retreat center in France. The discussion focused on Ephesians 6:12, where the apostle Paul states "our struggle is not against flesh and blood, but against the rulers, against the authorities, against the powers of this dark world and against the spiritual forces of evil in the heavenly realms."

One of the participants was an African pastor who was pursuing a doctorate in a French university. After the discussion he surprised me with this question: "Do you *really* believe in a world of spirits?"

"Of course," I answered. "Don't you?"

"Certainly," he replied, "but I'm black. Generally white people don't believe those things."

I must admit that for years I was one of those white people who did not take the realities of the unseen world seriously, even though I believed in spirit beings. My seminary training gave me an adequate understanding of the theology of angels, but that knowledge was mainly academic.

All that would change. When we sailed for France as missionaries, little did my wife and I realize how woefully unprepared we were for what we would encounter. We knew that France had the reputation of being one of the most rationalistic countries on the globe, but we were unaware of the occultism that was prevalent nearly everywhere. We soon began to realize that France's spiritual darkness was far more ominous than we had imagined.

Our shock of reality occurred when two men dressed in black appeared one day at our door. By that time we had secured a medieval castle that we had turned into a Bible center through which we had begun to reach into the lives of young people. After a long silence the men announced that the father of one of our young people, a man who was a professing Christian, had been found hanged in the woods, naked, with his open Bible by his side. I was being asked to have his funeral.

Before the body was transported to southern France for the service and the burial, a brief outdoor memorial was held for local friends and acquaintances. Shortly after this service began, the heavens broke loose. Bolts of lightning, deafening thunder, and torrential rains forced people to find shelter.

After that distressing experience we traveled to the place of the burial where a home was made available for my wife and me to spend the night. During the night I was awakened by an oppressive presence in the room that began to taunt me with voices in my mind. This presence made it known that he and his cohorts had been in France for centuries and mocked me for thinking I could make any inroads against their forces. The message was plain: we should get out of France and go back to where we belonged.

The remainder of the night was a struggle, spent in intense prayer. Finally, victory came, and thankfully our Lord was honored at the funeral service. That experience, however, became a turning point in my ministry. From that day on I realized that mission consists not only of confronting people with the gospel, but also confronting the spiritual forces of evil through prayer, all while claiming our position in Christ, high above every evil authority in the unseen world.

That experience was also the beginning of a long personal journey through the Scriptures, seeking to examine and to reflect deeply on the passages where the Lord has allowed us to peer into this mysterious world of the unseen. The journey filled me with awe as I began to gain insights into the wonder of God's unfolding plan of redemption.

This book is an attempt to share some of those insights. As noted earlier, the theme for these pages is the story of three princes. The first prince exercised his authority during a period that was woefully brief—perhaps only a few days. He was a human being and his name was Adam; he is the father of everyone reading these words.

The second seized authority as a usurper. A usurper is someone who assumes authority illegally. This prince is a spirit being that we commonly know as Satan, the adversary. Although he has since lost all legitimacy, he continues to exert incredible power as history's supreme vandal, shamelessly squatting on our spiritual inheritance.

The third Prince triumphed over Satan and regained everything that the first prince had forfeited. This Prince is the Son of God Himself. Though fully God, He had to assume humanity and prevail as a man. Jesus, called the "last Adam," had to win back what the first man had lost, and He had to do it on the same playing field. He is already crowned in heavenly places as King of all kings, but before establishing His earthly kingdom by force He is giving mankind the opportunity to enter His kingdom freely, through personal choice.

Let me conclude this introduction with some practical recommendations.

Any discussion of the world of spirits will necessitate avoiding extremes. We have already alluded to the first one—either believing and living as if the unseen world does not exist, or treating the world of spirits in much the same way that deists treat God—so far away that He never gets involved in their lives.

The second extreme is the exact opposite—allowing the existence of the spirit world to become a preoccupying obsession, or to attribute everything bad to demonic activity. The devil is not personally responsible for all our problems, even though he might like to be. We have to deal with the world and the flesh as well as the devil. Though the three work as a very effective team, they are not the same.

There is a third extreme which, in my opinion, is the most serious of all. In an effort to make the spiritual battle real, which of course it is, some seem to lower God almost to the level of the tribal gods of the pagans, not completely in control of the universe He has created. They do this because they seem to feel compelled to give God a way out with respect to the problem of evil. A Frenchman stated in my presence, "If there is a God, I hope He has a good excuse." What blasphemy! To be sure, the problem of evil is the fundamental problem of life, but in our quest for answers to this perplexing question, we must not reduce God to our feeble level of understanding. We must not "darken [his] counsel with words without knowledge" (Job 38:2). God is in control, but He is not the author of evil.

Throughout this book we will attempt to distinguish between what the Bible clearly *affirms*, on the one hand, and what we *infer* from God's revelation, on the other hand. You will have to use your own judgment concerning the validity of the assumptions you find. Whatever your conclusions might be, however, I can assure you that you are embarking on a fascinating journey.

The following pages will contain an abundance of Scripture references. Some of these references, as well as the concepts they teach, will be repeated several times. The repetition is intentional. We hope they will remind us again and again that as ambassadors for Christ, seated with Him in heavenly places, we are given spiritual authority over the powers of the unseen world. Let's not forget that though the devil commandeers a horde of fallen angels, he is neither omniscient nor omnipresent. We outrank the devil and the entire host of his evil powers.

# Chapter One

# A Prince
# for the
# New World

*God created the earth to be the dwelling place of man. Adam, created in God's image as the highest of all creation, was placed upon the earth as its prince. Angelic beings were created to be the invisible servants of God, serving mankind.*

GOD TOLD THE PATRIARCH JOB THAT ALL THE ANGELS shouted for joy when He laid the foundation of the earth (Job 38:7). We are not told whether they were assembled as spectators, as in a vast amphitheater, or as God's instruments, executing the Creator's orders. Nor do we know whether they were newly created, or whether they were summoned from the far-flung recesses of the universe. The focus of their attention was a minuscule speck of matter called Earth. Though the spectacle they were about to behold would fill them with wonder, they little realized that the consummate drama of all eternity was beginning.

The tiny earth was formless and empty, but suddenly, as the angels peered through the thick darkness, the voice of God thundered, and the earth was flooded with light. Day after day decrees were issued from the throne of God. In rapid succession the sky appeared, then land, soon clothed with every imaginable kind of vegetation.

The sun, the moon, and the stars appeared in the sky, and the sea and sky began to teem with life—every kind of sea animal, every kind of flying beast. Soon the land was covered with moving creatures, running, crawling, jumping.

## The God of creation is infinite

Whenever the Christian philosopher Francis Schaeffer spoke of God, he usually prefaced his remarks with two adjectives: infinite and personal.

From the beginning of time men and angels have been awed by the *infinity* of God. No sensitive person can venture into the out-of-doors without being stunned by the infinite diversity of God's creation. An eminent biologist was once asked where he had gone on his vacation. His answer was, "Halfway across my garden. And next year I intend to continue my journey."

It has not been until our present generation, however, that we have even begun to apprehend the fabulous vastness and complexity of God's world. Who would have dreamed, even a few generations ago, that in observable space there are at least an estimated 200 billion galaxies, each containing some 200 billion stars? Such numbers cause many to believe that the number of known stars is many times greater than the number of grains of sand on all the beaches of the world.

*Or who would have thought it unlikely that any two snow crystals (not ice particles), out of all those made over the entire history of the planet, have ever looked completely alike? The mathematical possibility for diversity in snowflakes is seemingly infinite.*

Or who would have imagined that the minuscule flagellum that propels certain cells of our body is attached to a complex rotary motor and propeller system of some forty interrelated parts rotating at 100,000 rpm? The removal of any one of the parts would cause the cell's system to cease functioning.

Could anyone have foreseen that a DNA molecule is comprised of chemical bases arranged in approximately three *billion* precise sequences, containing enough information to fill all the books of any of the world's largest libraries? The ability for those molecules to instantly communicate this information to other molecules baffles even the most brilliant scientific minds.

It certainly does not require a leap of faith to believe that our world is the product of an infinite, intelligent Creator. No one has ever come close to explaining how all this could possibly be the result of impersonal time and chance.

For this reason the most colossal affront to God is to claim that His fabulous world and all it contains came about without a designer. That must cause the angels to shake their heads in disbelief. Even the most sophisticated

> *God is both infinite and personal*

man of science would find it unthinkable to offend his little child by pretending that the crude drawing of a heart with the words, "I love you, daddy," just happened to come about when the child accidentally dropped her paper and crayon on the floor.

> The heavens declare the glory of God; the skies proclaim the work of his hands. Day after day they pour forth speech; night after night they display knowledge. There is no speech or language where their voice is not heard. Their voice goes out into all the earth, their words to the ends of the world (Psalm 19:1-4).

Where there is design there must be a designer.

### The God of creation is personal

Yes, the angels shouted for joy as they watched the infinite God make the land and the sea, the sky and the earth, and every kind of plant and animal life. But no angel among the myriads of heavenly beings was prepared for what came next. The Creator's words shattered their angelic imaginations. Were they understanding correctly? And yet... this is what they heard:

> Let us make man in our image, in our likeness (Genesis 1:26).

So God created mankind in his own image, in the image of God he created him; male and female he created them (Genesis 1:27).

> ## Adam was a person, having historic identity

Man? Then woman? In the image of the Creator? What could this mean? From the dust of the earth God made man. From the rib of the man, God made woman. A cosmic gasp must have filled the universe as the angels covered their faces in disbelief.

Adam was created as a fully-developed person, having historic identity—the kind of history lived out in time and space on planet Earth. From his side God created woman, also a person, distinct from Adam. She too was fully developed, immediately capable of procreation. Had we known their language, we would have been able to listen in on their first conversation and understand what they were saying.

No matter what we understand about the creation of man, we must never lose sight of these two biblical realities: 1) he was created directly by a personal God, from the dust of the earth and not from lower forms of life, and 2) he was created as a fully developed being. Adam is not some kind of poetic symbol of humanity. If you are going to take the Bible seriously, you cannot have it any other way. Further, if you do not take this part of the Bible seriously, everything that follows will unravel.

We worship a God who is both *infinite* and *personal*.

> For since the creation of the world God's invisible qualities—His eternal power and divine nature—have been clearly seen, being understood from what has been made, *so that men are without excuse* (Romans 1:20, emphasis added).

### In the likeness of God

Of everything that God the Creator made, man alone was created in God's image. What does that mean, and just what does it tell us about God?

It is obvious that we are not talking about a physical image. Though God can appear to men in a visible form, and though God the Son later took upon Himself the body of a man, the likeness between God and Adam is not to be seen in Adam's physical appearance. The physical characteristics attributed to God that we read about in the Scriptures are merely figures of speech to help us better understand His dealings with mankind.

> *God breathed spirituality into Adam*

The likeness of man to God is found in man's personality. God is a person. Man is a person.

Personality is an elusive concept. It is usually defined by such things as self-consciousness and freedom of choice. Personality traits are all related to one thing, however—the spirit. They are spiritual qualities. God is Spirit. Though God breathed into animals the breath of life, making them living beings, it was only into man that He breathed spirituality—*the capacity to rise above time and space in his perception of reality.*

Animals have instinct, but they do not experience spirituality. We might call cows contented, but that term has no meaning when compared with human satisfaction. I was once invited by a Pennsylvania farmer to see his champion Holstein cow, the global winner for milk production in that particular year. She was a beast of amazing proportions, never allowed to roam the fields, confined day and night to her pen where her nourishment was scientifically measured. She was surrounded by blue ribbons and trophies. Jokingly I made a statement that, to my surprise, caused my farmer friend no little distress. I said, "Do you think all these trophies make this cow any more contented than all the other cows in your herd?" This bothered him during the remainder of our time together.

Spirituality meant that Adam could *know* that he was a man, that he was made by God, that he was morally responsible, that he had the freedom to make choices, and that he was placed upon this earth to fulfill a mission. From man's spirituality flow all the qualities that distinguish him from beasts: the ability to love or hate, to create or destroy, to know both ecstasy and deep depression, to be noble or to be vile.

## Made to rule

Now we come to the main point of this chapter. God did not create man merely to allow him to enjoy the beautiful earth. He was given a mission. It was God's plan that the earth would be ruled by man. Angels were made to serve; man was made to reign.

> *Adam was created to be a prince*

Adam was created to be a prince. His kingdom was the earth. He was appointed ruler over God's new world.

This is made clear in the Genesis account. The Scriptures reveal the mission of man both before and after his creation. Before creating Adam, God said,

> Let us make man in our image, in our likeness, and let them *rule* over the fish of the sea and the birds of the air, over the livestock over all the earth, and over all the creatures that move along the ground (Genesis 1:26, emphasis added).

After creating Adam, God formally commissioned him.

> Be fruitful and increase in number; fill the earth and subdue it. *Rule* [have dominion] over the fish of the sea and the birds of the air and over every living creature that moves on the ground (Genesis 1:28, emphasis added).

Adam was commissioned not only to be fruitful, to increase in number, and to fill the earth—he was to subdue it. He was to *rule* over every living creature.

Look at Psalm 8:3-8, later quoted in Hebrews 2:6-8 (emphasis added):

> When I consider your heavens, the work of your fingers, the moon and the stars, which you have set in place, what is man that you are mindful of him, the son of man that you

care for him? You made him a little lower than the heavenly beings and crowned him with glory and honor. *You made him ruler over the works of your hands; you put everything under his feet:* all flocks and herds, and the beasts of the field, the birds of the air, and the fish in the sea, all that swim the paths of the seas.

*In God's sovereign plan, the world was to be ruled by man, the only being created in God's image. This was a legal contract between God and Adam, for whatever God decrees becomes law. It was sealed in the courts of heaven. Only one being in the entire universe could break this contract. His name was Adam.* That fact is fundamental in understanding the drama of mankind.

Adam and Eve enjoyed perfect contentment in a perfect environment. They did not realize, however, that they were not alone with the animals of God's new world. Though they were able to perceive only what was visible, their every move was scrutinized by another being, one who was incredibly intelligent and powerful.

The rule of the new world's prince would be pathetically brief. It would come to an end in an unspeakable tragedy, usurped by a being later known as Satan. To understand this tragedy, we must look beyond the veil of the visible and peer into the mysterious events occurring in the unseen world.

## Discussion questions:

What does the creation teach us about the nature of God?

What is the essence of spirituality, and how does it manifest itself in everyday life?

What do we mean when we say that Adam was the *legal* prince of this world?

# Chapter Two

# High Treason

*God appointed Lucifer, the highest of angelic beings, to be Adam's protector. Filled with jealousy that a physically weak being should occupy the place he thought should be rightfully his, Satan developed in his warped mind a plot to secure dominion over the earth. This led to a second plot: Not only would he seek to be the earth's prince, but he would also make a play for the very throne of God by pitting God's love against His justice. All this represented high treason. Lucifer, the morning star, became Satan, the adversary.*

PEACE AND HARMONY REIGNED WHEN THE EARTH HAD ITS beginnings. There was unity in the heavenly courts, for "*all* the angels shouted for joy" (Job 38:7, emphasis added). Further, we are told that at the end of the six days of creation, God saw *all* that He had made, and it was *very good* (Genesis 1:31).

Yet when we open our Bibles to chapter 3 of Genesis, the most tragic chapter of the entire Bible, we immediately realize that something had already gone terribly wrong.

Appearing in the midst of the beauty and harmony of the garden, a serpent approached Eve and began to talk. When we hear the word

15

serpent, we think of a slithering creature that generally strikes fear into the heart of those who see it. Eve's reaction would indicate that this was not the kind of animal she encountered; she did not flee. The serpent in the garden was certainly a different animal from the serpents we know about. Jewish tradition says that the serpent originally walked upright. The Genesis account states that it was God's curse that condemned the serpent to crawl on its belly and taste dust.

> *The talking serpent was the tool of a powerful spirit*

Further, Eve's lack of astonishment about a talking serpent should not surprise us. Let's not forget that though she was a fully-developed human being, she was probably only days old. Since Eve had not yet conceived her first child (Genesis 4:1), the lapse of time between the creation and the fall was woefully short. During those few days she had had so many incredible experiences that absolutely nothing would have amazed her.

In her innocence she did not realize that the talking serpent was the tool of a powerful spirit. Nor did she grasp the blasphemous nature of his words. In her seduction Eve became the victim of treason of the highest order, treason against the Creator by one of His highest creations.

Who was this spirit? How did he get into the garden? What provoked his rebellion against his Creator and his unspeakable wickedness?

In Revelation 12 the "ancient serpent" is clearly identified as the devil (the accuser), or Satan (the adversary), "who leads the whole world astray" (v. 9). The mighty spirit who spoke to Eve would dominate human history from that time on until his ultimate defeat in the lake of fire (Revelation 20:10).

## Two intriguing passages

Though the malicious influence of Satan overshadows the entire story of mankind, the name "Satan" occurs only in four Old Testament books: 1 Chronicles, Job, Psalms, and Zechariah. Further, of the 19 times the term "Satan" appears, 14 of them are in the first two chapters of Job. The term "devil" does not even appear in the entire Old Testament. It is in the New Testament that his identity and nature are fully revealed.

But though Satan is only rarely *named* in the Old Testament, two intriguing passages are generally identified with him. The passages are allegorical—they are descriptions of one thing under the image of another. The first is in Isaiah 14. In this passage, which begins as a taunt against the king of Babylon, we read in verses 12 through 15:

> How you have fallen from heaven, O morning star, son of the dawn! You have been cast down to the earth, you who once laid low the nations! You said in your heart, "I will ascend to heaven; I will raise my throne above the stars of God; I will sit enthroned on the mount of assembly, on the utmost heights of the sacred mountain. I will ascend above the tops of the clouds; I will make myself like the Most High." But you are brought down to the grave, to the depths of the pit.

A similar passage is in Ezekiel 28:12-19. This passage begins as a reference to the prince of Tyre, then moves on to Tyre's king. But again, the language of the passage leads us to see it as a springboard to someone far more mysterious and sinister than an earthly ruler. Look at some of the phrases in these verses.

> "You were the model of perfection, full of wisdom and perfect in beauty" (v. 12).
> "You were in Eden, the garden of God" (v. 13).
> "You were anointed as a guardian cherub, for so I ordained you" (v. 14).
> "You were blameless in your ways from the day you were created till wickedness was found in you. Through your widespread trade you were filled with violence, and you sinned. So I drove you in disgrace from the mount of God,

and I expelled you, O guardian cherub, from among the fiery stones" (vv. 15-16).

These passages in Isaiah and Ezekiel do not mention Satan by name, which means that we can only assume that they refer to him. It is obvious, however, that the words describe a being far different from an earthly ruler. The passages make no sense when we see them as a description of the earthly rulers mentioned. Through the centuries Bible scholars have believed that they give us valuable insights into Satan's origin, mission, and sin, as well as his defeat by the archangel Michael, depicted in Revelation 12, where he and his angels are cast out of the heavenly realms once for all.

> *Angels were created to be God's messengers*

If we assume that these passages provide information concerning Satan, what can we learn from them?

## Satan's origin

Satan, called Lucifer or the morning star in Isaiah 14, is one of the myriads of spiritual beings we call angels, a word which means messenger. Angels are created beings. They are spirits who play a dominant role in God's administration of His creation, perhaps with a particular mission to the earth. We read in Psalm 103:20-21: "Praise the LORD, you his angels, you mighty ones who do his bidding, who obey his word. Praise the LORD, all his heavenly hosts, you his servants who do his will."

As created beings, angels are finite, and like man, they were given freedom. Thus they were capable of rebellion. Peter tells us that angels sinned (2 Peter 2:4), and Jude speaks of angels who did not keep their positions of authority (Jude 6).

Various passages of Scripture indicate that there is an angelic hierarchy, with certain of them occupying positions of greater power than others, such as Michael the archangel. An intriguing passage in Daniel 10 reveals the mysterious truth that angelic princes in the spirit world exercise influence over entire kingdoms in the political world.

Though Satan, as an angelic being, is a part of God's creation, we must not conclude that God created a being who was evil at the time of his creation. At his creation Lucifer was perfect, without sin or rebellion. In Ezekiel 28:12 we read, "You were the model of perfection, full of wisdom and perfect in beauty." Later the text tells us that he was blameless from the day he was created until wickedness was found in him (v. 15).

## Satan's mission and fall

Some Bible scholars have proposed that this exalted spiritual being that we call Lucifer, the morning star, was in ages past given authority over a pre-Adamic earth, and that, lifted up with pride, he rebelled against his Creator, plunging this earth into darkness and confusion. They believe that there is a time gap between verses 1 and 2 of the first chapter of Genesis, and that Lucifer became Satan ages before the Genesis account of creation.

This hypothesis, however, presents a number of problems. We have pointed out that at the end of the sixth day, God looked at His creation and pronounced that *all* that He had made was very good. The statement that the earth was without form and empty in no way implies that it was morally corrupted by some cosmic rebellion before the six days of creation. It simply means that it was not yet habitable. There was work to be done during the six days.

The passage we read in Ezekiel offers some fascinating insights concerning the time of Lucifer's rebellion. Ezekiel 28:13 states, "You were in Eden, the garden of God." In verse 14: "You were anointed as a guardian cherub, for so I ordained you." In verses 15-17:

> You were blameless in your ways from the day you were created till wickedness was found in you. Through your widespread trade you were filled with violence, and you sinned. So I drove you in disgrace from the mount of God, and I expelled you, O guardian cherub, from among the fiery stones.

19

Is the Eden mentioned in Ezekiel, called the garden of God, the same as the Garden of Eden of Genesis 1-3? It certainly seems to be. If we are willing to assume that the Ezekiel passage indeed refers to the Garden of Eden, many things fall into place.

> *Lucifer was the "guardian cherub" of Adam*

*First,* we might infer that Lucifer was appointed by God to be the "guardian cherub" of Adam and Eve (Ezekiel 28:14). The term "cherub" (cherubim in the plural) is a designation of a certain category of angelic beings, appointed by God as guardians. Was Lucifer's mission, therefore, to watch over Adam, the one appointed to be the prince of God's new creation? The need for this protection was certainly related to man's physical vulnerability as a human being.

Thus, it may well be that Lucifer, perhaps the most exalted of angelic beings, was appointed to be the guardian of Adam, the most exalted of God's earthly creations.

*Second,* that Lucifer was lifted up with pride and jealousy against Adam, this physically vulnerable human being, limited by time and space and a one-dimensional perception of God's world. "What was God thinking," Lucifer may have mused, "in giving this weakling authority over the earth, when I am the one who should be ruling?" Lucifer quickly lost the sense of his own mission and began to covet the mission of man.

*Third,* that as Lucifer began to ponder seizing the authority given by God to Adam, something infinitely more sinister began to fill his mind, a thought that would fill the universe with utter horror. Why not make a play for the very throne of God?

> You said in your heart, "I will ascend to heaven; I will raise my throne above the stars of God; I will sit enthroned on the mount of assembly, on the utmost heights of the sacred mountain. I will ascend above the tops of the clouds; I will make myself like the Most High" (Isaiah 14:13-14).

As one of God's highest and most intelligent creations, Lucifer knew a great deal about God. He knew that God was absolutely *righteous* and *just*. These attributes are the foundation of God's throne (Psalm 89:14).

Satan also knew that man, who was created in God's image, was the object of God's eternal *love*. Satan knew that if God violated either His righteousness or His love, His right to rule would be compromised, endangering His very authority. The attributes of God are not just personality traits; they are essential qualities of His very being. "If I can only cause this despicable creature to rebel against his creator, perhaps everything will become mine," he must have thought.

By the time this scheme had come together in his fiendish mind, Lucifer was no longer the morning star. He had become Satan the adversary, the prince of darkness.

## Discussion questions:

Does God's foreknowledge make Him responsible for evil?

Why is freedom a prerequisite for both good and evil?

How did Satan create an apparently irresolvable dilemma for God?

# Chapter Three

# Cosmic Upheaval

*To achieve his fiendish plan, Satan, embodying a serpent, deceived Eve and tempted her to eat of the forbidden fruit. Adam made no effort to stop her and willfully rebelled against the command of his Creator by accepting the fruit from her hand. The result was the death of mankind—both physical and spiritual separation from God. That disobedience brought devastating consequences upon all of creation. It also meant that Satan, by subjecting man to himself, became the legal prince of this world.*

THE ANGELS WHO SHOUTED FOR JOY WHEN GOD LAID THE foundations of the earth would all too quickly be filled with grief. Because Eve had not yet conceived her first child, only a short amount of time could have elapsed between the creation of man and his sin. David's affirmation in Psalm 51:5, "Surely I was sinful at birth, sinful from the time my mother conceived me," has been a reality from the very beginning of the human race. Every human being, with the exception of our Lord, has been morally flawed from conception, having inherited spiritual death.

### The temptation of Eve

Satan's temptation of Eve was a masterpiece of seduction. It occurred in three steps.

*First,* he sowed doubts in her mind concerning the command of God, causing her to magnify the prohibition. "Did God *really* say that you could not eat from this one tree of the garden? Are you sure that your husband heard correctly? Stop and think—does it make sense that God wouldn't allow you to take one little bite out of what I am holding out to you? After all, didn't He put you in charge down here? Come on!"

> *Eve's temptation was a masterpiece of seduction*

We do not know how many varieties of trees were in the garden, nor can we imagine their delightful taste before the Fall. Eve knew she could eat from every tree except one, but Satan apparently succeeded in making her forget all the others. You can almost hear her saying to herself, like billions of her descendants, "You can't do *anything* in this garden." She even played along with the serpent, saying, "We cannot even touch it," magnifying the prohibition.

*Second,* he flatly contradicted God's command, affirming his own authority above that of God. "You will *not* die." It is not possible for us to fathom the infinite implications of this hideous statement. This is the first *recorded* incident in all of eternity in which one of God's creations willfully opposed His authority. It was the first shot fired in the cosmic revolution against God.

If there was anything crystal clear in God's communication with Adam, it was that the penalty for disobedience was death. "And the Lord commanded the man, 'You are free to eat from any tree in the garden; but you must not eat from the tree of the knowledge of good and evil, for when you eat of it you will certainly die'" (Genesis 2:16-17). Satan was fully aware of God's command and the consequences if he disobeyed.

*Third*, he offered Eve moral autonomy. "For God knows that when you eat from it your eyes will be opened, and you will be *like* God, knowing good and evil" (Genesis 3:5, emphasis added).

Satan's statement does not imply in any way that Eve would become like God in His essence, all powerful or all knowing. He was tempting her to loosen herself from God's authority and become morally independent. The Hebrew verb "to know" implies knowledge by experience and in this context carries with it the idea of ownership. The very act of eating this fruit would be a statement to God that she was capable of making her own decisions, no matter what her husband had told her about God's commands.

> *Adam rebelled willfully against his Creator*

Satan's words put desire into Eve's heart. She saw that the fruit of the tree was "*good for food.*" Her mouth began to water. The more she looked at it, the more she wanted it. It was "*pleasing to the eye.*" She wanted to affirm her own independence, for she saw that it was "*desirable for gaining wisdom*" (Genesis 3:6, emphasis added).

Though thousands of years would pass before the apostle John would write about "the lust of the flesh, the lust of the eyes, and the pride of life" (1 John 2:16, KJV), Satan, without any previous experience, had already aroused those desires and become the master of seduction.

Eve took some of the fruit and ate. Then she gave some to her husband, who was with her, and he ate it. You can almost hear Satan's fiendish cry of victory. With this act of disobedience God's creation was shaken to the core. From that time on nothing would be the same.

## The sin of Adam

The sin of Adam was fundamentally different from the sin of his wife. Eve sinned through deception. She was seduced by Satan. 1 Timothy 2:14 says, "Adam was not the one deceived; it was the woman who was deceived and became a sinner." Adam sinned *willfully*, knowing full well the consequences of his act. He was the one who personally had been given the commandment, and there would have been no question in his mind about whether he had heard correctly.

It is for this reason that Adam, not Eve, is held responsible for the fall of the human race. Paul makes this clear in Romans 5:12: "Sin entered the world through one man, and death through sin, and in this way death came to all people."

> *Sin is to transform freedom into independence*

Adam sinned in the most cowardly and despicable manner possible. The text makes it clear that he was *with his wife* when she took the forbidden fruit (Genesis 3:6). He allowed her to partake of the fruit of the tree with no apparent effort to stop her. Can it be that Adam, the protector of Eve, was willing to sacrifice his wife in order to assert his own independence from his Creator? We men find it hard to be proud of our first father.

What was the essence of the first sin, and of every sin committed since that fateful day—by you, by me, and by every human being? *It was to transform freedom into independence.* God had given to mankind the priceless gift of freedom. Man's freedom was and is real; it is not an illusion. But freedom is always defined by its limitations. Even God is limited by His nature.

Yet freedom is only one step away from independence. In affirming his independence, man spiritually alienated himself from his Creator. This is death.

Genesis 3 reveals the answer to the problem of evil, which has been the fundamental enigma of humanity from the beginning of time. Is God responsible for evil? No! Is evil eternal? No! Is evil an illusion? Absolutely not! Evil entered God's beautiful world through deliberate choice: first that of Lucifer, then that of Adam. *The essence of evil is independence from the one in whom we live and move and have our being* (Acts 17:28).

## Satan, the new prince

Satan's strategy was two-fold: first, overthrowing Adam as prince of the world, and second, seeking to topple God from His throne. In causing man to sin, Satan achieved the first part of his strategy; he would never achieve the second.

By shifting Adam's allegiance from God to himself, *Satan obtained legal authority over the kingdoms of the world.* The moment Adam aligned himself with Satan's lies, putting himself under the authority of the devil, he fell from his position of God-given authority. It was at this instant that Satan rose to become the new reigning prince.

> *Satan becomes the new reigning prince*

This is graphically portrayed in the account of the temptation of Christ. When Satan led Jesus to a high mountain to see the kingdoms of the world, he stated: "I will give you all their authority and splendor; it has been *given* [or *handed over*] to me, and I can give it to anyone I want to. If you worship me, it will all be yours" (Luke 4:6-7, emphasis added). The giver could be none other than God himself. Jesus did not contest this statement. Three times He called him the prince of this world (John 12:31, 14:30, 16:11). John stated that the whole world was under the control of the evil one (1 John 5:19).

## The death of mankind

Satan, however, would rule over a ruined kingdom. It is doubtful that even Satan was able to foresee the magnitude of the consequences of the fall of man, The consequences were immediate and brutal. God's warning to Adam had been unequivocal. Eating the forbidden fruit brought immediate death, and the consequences of death affected every aspect of man, his relationships, and even the created world. Paul states that, "the whole creation has been groaning as in the pains of childbirth right up to the present time" (Romans 8:22).

Death is essentially separation—separation from God, the source of life (John 1:4). Death should not be seen primarily as a punishment, but as an inevitable consequence. Its effects are both physical and spiritual.

*Physical death* is separation that takes place within man himself, resulting in the disintegration of his very being. The immediate consequence is physical sickness. The final consequence is the total separation of the spirit from the body (James 2:26).

> The essence
> of death is
> separation

*Spiritual death* is the separation of man from God. Just as the immediate consequence of physical death is physical sickness, the immediate consequence of spiritual death is moral sickness. Moral sickness manifests itself in the sinful nature (Romans 7:14-18), which the Bible calls the *flesh,* the source of temptation to do evil.

The sinful nature finds its roots in the subconscious, the domain of the mind that is not consciously subject to the will. The sinful nature attracts and seduces the will, causing sin to be conceived (James 1:13-15). The final consequence of spiritual death is eternal separation from God in the lake of fire, which is the second death (Revelation 20:14).

All have sinned. The proof of this is that death has been passed on to all people (Romans 5:12, 1 Corinthians 15:21-22, Ephesians 2:1-3). Sin entered the world by one man and death by sin. The Bible does not say that we are *guilty* of the sin of Adam; however, the universality of death proves that all mankind has been affected by Adam's sin.

## The immediate effects of mankind's death

Years would pass before Adam would experience the ultimate physical reality of his death. According to the Genesis account, Adam lived to be 930 years old before he left this earth (Genesis 5:5). The immediate effects of death were brutal. However, those effects would haunt him during all of his 930 years on earth.

First came the birth of shame (Genesis 3:7). Immediately upon eating the fruit, the eyes of Adam and Eve were opened to something they had not known before—the shame of their nakedness. This speaks of the disharmony, or disintegration, within their very beings. Before the fall they were complete persons, the body and the spirit functioning in perfect harmony. When sin came, the body ceased being an expression of the spirit, but instead became an object of carnal desire.

Second came the experience of guilt and alienation from their Creator (Genesis 3:8-10). When God approached Adam and Eve, they were filled with fear and guilt and attempted to hide themselves. "Where are you?" God spoke. Adam's answer is revealing: "I heard you in the garden, and I was afraid because I was naked; so I hid." He did not say he was hiding because he had sinned; he was hiding because he had been caught. He was experiencing a feeling of guilt for the very first time, and he did not like it.

Third came the refusal of responsibility (Genesis 3:11-13). Adam and Eve did not deny their sin; they simply did not want to take responsibility for it. Freedom and responsibility must always go together, but both Adam and Eve responded as if they were victims rather than responsible beings. Rather than confessing, they made excuses.

While we might have some sympathy for Eve, who admits that she was deceived by the serpent, Adam's statement is deplorable. It is completely in line with the cowardly nature of his sin. Not only did he blame his wife for something that he willfully did, he even blamed God for giving her to him.

All this leads to the severe judgment of God (Genesis 3:14-24). The serpent was cursed to crawl on its belly and to eat dust. Eve was cursed with agony in childbearing and subjection to her husband. Adam was cursed with a hostile creation which would bring suffering and eventually physical death. God's judgment culminated in the expulsion of Adam and Eve from the beautiful garden, thereafter guarded by cherubim with flaming swords, preventing them from access to the Tree of Life.

## *The mystery of redemption*

If we allow ourselves to reflect deeply upon the Genesis account of God's judgments, sooner or later we will be struck by a stunning omission. In all the curses God pronounces, none are precisely directed to the very one who was responsible for beginning the tragedy, Satan himself. God cursed the serpent, but the serpent was a part of the animal world. God brought judgment against Adam and Eve, and even creation itself, but nothing is specifically directed against Satan. To be sure, Satan's *ultimate* fate is clearly predicted, but why does he personally escape God's *immediate* curse?

This omission seems incomprehensible until we fully realize that through man's rebellion, the world now has a new prince, Satan himself. By willfully refusing the authority of God, Adam had unwittingly put himself under the authority of Satan. *If God had cursed Satan before stripping him of his authority at the cross, He would have compromised the redemption of Adam and Eve, and of all mankind.*

Let's review. When God created the world, He gave it to man as his property. What God decrees becomes inviolable law. Adam was made prince, but in the cosmic upheaval that followed, that title went to Satan through Adam's submission to Satan's authority. Satan's revolt brought the Creator face-to-face with two choices: mankind's redemption or his ultimate destruction.

In a Bible discussion related to Satan's rebellion, a young woman asked, "Why doesn't God squash Satan like a bug?" The answer, of course, is that God could. But in doing so, much more would be squashed than Satan, for if Satan had been immediately consigned to the lake of fire, so would Adam and Eve, thus ending all hope of redemption. If by man came death, by man had to come the resurrection of the dead, according to the statement of the apostle Paul (1 Corinthians 15:21).

*A man had to gain back what the first man had lost, and he had to do it as a man.*

All this gives context to the first great redemptive promise of the Bible, Genesis 3:15. Speaking to the serpent, but most certainly addressing His words to the spirit of evil responsible for the serpent's act, God says, "I will put enmity between you and the woman, and between your offspring and hers; he will crush your head, and you will strike his heel."

Words difficult to understand? Of course. But there can be no doubt concerning the identity of the woman's offspring. "When the set time had fully come, God sent his Son, born of a woman, born under the law, to redeem those under the law, that we might receive the full rights of sons" (Galatians 4:4-5).

Satan's head would indeed be crushed, but at tremendous cost to God.

Did Satan understand those words? He could not have known their full import. Perhaps he saw them as a pathetic statement of a Creator who was bound by His own justice. But these words were the opening shot of God's secret strategy, a strategy hidden from the prince of darkness until Jesus kicked open the gates of Hades from the inside and publicly stripped Satan of all legal authority, sealing his fate forever.

For Adam, though, those words must have brought a glimmer of hope. No longer lashing out against the one God had given him, Adam turned to his wife in that moment and called her Eve, because she would become the mother of all the living.

As a foretaste of what was to follow, God took away the leaves that the first couple had sewn together to cover their nakedness and clothed them with the skin of animals, perhaps still dripping with blood, without which "there is no forgiveness of sin" (Hebrews 9:22).


## Discussion questions:

In what way did Eve become "like" God in eating the forbidden fruit?

Why is Adam and not Eve held accountable for man's rebellion against God?

What is death, and why is it the inevitable consequence of independence from God?

# Chapter Four

# Full-Scale Rebellion

*From Adam to Christ the history of mankind is an endless cycle of rebellion and judgment. God's severe measures can be explained only by the fact that the pervasive demonic influence could not be stopped except by the annihilation of entire populations. This influence spread through idolatry, occult practices, and sexual perversion.*

BY THE TIME ADAM AND EVE HAD BEEN EXPELLED FROM God's beautiful garden, Satan had achieved his first goal. He had become the prince of this world. Unlike earthly princes, however, he did not set up his throne with great pomp and ceremony and proclaim his glory throughout the world. His was a kingdom which was silent and unseen.

Satan would never achieve his second goal. He would never ascend to the throne of the universe. Though he would spread his power everywhere throughout the world, he would never be able to break away from the restraints of his Creator.

Nowhere else in the Bible is this more clear than in the book of Job, perhaps the earliest book of the Bible. The story of Job is one of those rare instances where the veil concealing the unseen world is stripped away. Here Satan is mentioned by name fourteen times.

Several facts become evident in the book of Job. First, Satan, as one of the angels, had access to the throne of God. God apparently was respectful of his judicial authority, even though this authority had been stolen from Adam. Second, Satan had the power and was granted the freedom to inflict unimaginable suffering on one of God's choice servants. Third, and most important, even though he was now the legitimate prince of this world, Satan's power was limited by God's overriding providence.

Job's miserable comforters, trying to explain everything from their limited human understanding, caused Job's suffering to go from bad to worse. We might find it surprising that even when God spoke with His servant Job, He did not choose to reveal the hidden drama of Job's suffering. Rather than responding to Job's inquiries, God overwhelmed Job with dozens of questions, many of them seemingly irrelevant from our viewpoint. Their implication, however, became clear. If Job was unable to explain the most obvious things, how could he hope to understand the mysteries that were hidden from his sight?

But when Job finally met God face to face, he was satisfied. No further explanation was needed.

## Satan's unholy horde

Though precise references to Satan are sparse in the rest of the Old Testament, his depraved influence overshadows everything. The entire Old Testament account of man's history is tragic, from the murder of Abel to the dispersion of God's chosen people. The Old Testament presents an unending cycle of rebellion and judgment: the flood, the tower of Babel, the pathetic stories of the patriarchs, the wandering in the desert, the atrocities of the period of the judges, the failures of the monarchy, the division of the kingdom. It takes little imagination to realize that the earth was under the domination of a prince who was the personification of evil.

Although he is one of the most powerful, if not *the* most powerful, of God's created angels, how can this being exercise such sweeping power over the entire earth? The answer is that he does not do it alone. When Satan rebelled, he generated a cosmic revolution, leading an innumerable host of angelic beings who chose to follow his revolt.

That a vast army of demons and fallen angels exists is a reality that no one who takes the Bible seriously can doubt. Why and when they rebelled against God is harder to pin down. Peter talks about the angels who sinned (2 Peter 2:4), and Jude speaks of angels who did not keep their positions of authority (Jude 6), but neither of these passages gives us an indication of when those events occurred, or what were the circumstances.

> *When Satan rebelled, he generated a cosmic revolution*

Revelation 12:3-4 comes closest to giving us an answer to the question. In the symbolism characteristic of that book, we read: "Then another sign appeared in heaven: an enormous red dragon with seven heads and ten horns and seven crowns on his heads. His tail swept a third of the stars out of the sky and flung them to the earth." We know from verse 9 that the enormous red dragon is none other than Satan, the devil, the ancient serpent. We know too that the term "star" is frequently used to designate angelic beings, as in Job 38:7 and Isaiah 14:12.

The Revelation passage leads us to believe that when Satan rebelled, he swept with him a third of the angelic beings, and that they have become the "kingdom of the air" of which he is the prince (Ephesians 2:2). We can only speculate concerning why and when these fallen angels rebelled against God, but again we stress that there is no evidence that the angelic revolt occurred ages before the Genesis account of the creation of the earth as some have thought. We have already emphasized several times that at the end of the sixth day, God pronounced that all was good in His creation.

Why did these angelic beings join with Satan in his rebellion? The most plausible explanation is that they were already under the authority of their chief, Lucifer, and that they were assigned with him to the earth to serve the posterity of Adam and Eve. Were they forced, against their will, to submit to their ruler and rebel against their Creator? Absolutely not! Imagining that they could have their own kingdom, they took the step that would seal their doom forever. There is nothing in the Scriptures promising redemption for fallen angels.

## Conflict in the unseen world is real

We have pointed out that the prophet Daniel reveals that at least some of the unseen spiritual rulers are assigned to political or national entities. When the angelic messenger was sent to the prophet Daniel in answer to his prayers, he stated:

Do not be afraid, Daniel. Since the first day that you set your mind to gain understanding and to humble yourself before your God, your words were heard, and I have come in response to them. But the prince of the Persian kingdom resisted me twenty-one days. Then Michael, one of the chief princes, came to help me, because I was detained there with the king of Persia (Daniel 10:12-13).

Then the angelic being says, "Soon I will return to fight against the prince of Persia, and when I go, the prince of Greece will come" (v. 20). Conflict in the unseen world is real.

When my wife and I were living in Macon, France, we invited our neighbors for tea one afternoon. In the course of the conversation the wife of the couple we had invited, knowing that we were there as missionaries, made a rather startling statement. "I can understand why your work is so difficult," she said. "Macon is under the authority of a *martinet*." (In French "martinet" is a term for a whip.) "He is a very powerful prince in the spiritual world. He is directly responsible to the prince of Lyon, the highest in all of France." Her husband's face turned ashen. I said, "I know from the Bible that there are different levels of power in the unseen world, but where did you learn it?" "It's in the books," she said. "It's all written in the books." Later her daughter came to me and said, "Don't listen to my mother.

She says things that she makes up." It was apparent, however, that our neighbor was not speaking from her imagination.

### Satan extends his kingdom

The story of the Old Testament is one of continuous tragedy: a cycle of rebellion and judgment. No sensitive person can read through the Old Testament without being shocked by the continual degradation of humanity and the seemingly merciless judgments of God, especially when we realize that God is a God of compassion and love. To read the Old Testament only in the context of its visible dimension poses almost insuperable perplexity in the mind of the reader. Why would a God of mercy order the extermination of entire peoples, not only men and women but also innocent children and even animals?

I suggest there is only one explanation for the severity and scope of those judgments. If God was ready to bring destruction upon the entire human race by a universal flood, if God poured down fire and brimstone on the cities of Sodom and Gomorrah, if God commanded the extermination of entire civilizations at the time of the conquest—and we could go on and on—there had to be more than meets the physical eye. We can only conclude that demonic activity was so prevalent, so profound, and so devastating that total destruction was the only possible remedy for such torment on this miserable earth. That is made evident in Deuteronomy 18:12, where it is stated that it was "because of these detestable practices the LORD [their] God [drove] out those nations before [them]."

> *Satan extends his kingdom through three tactics*

What is the strategy of Satan and his unholy angels for extending their kingdom? Three tactics stand out. Two are explicitly identified in the Scriptures; the third is there by implication. The three are idolatry, various forms of occultism, and illicit sexual activity. Each of these practices has the potential of bringing people into direct contact with unclean spirits with the accompanying potential of demonic control.

First, *idolatry.* Nothing was more prevalent among the ancient civilizations than rampant idolatry of all forms. Believing in many gods, the people seemed to be willing to fall down and worship any visible representation of false divinities, no matter how ridiculous such worship might be. One of the most ludicrous accounts of this practice is found in Isaiah 44:16-18, describing a man who fabricates an idol:

> Half of the wood he burns in the fire; over it he prepares his meal, he roasts his meat, and eats his fill. He also warms himself and says, 'Ah! I am warm; I see the fire.' From the rest he makes a god, his idol; he bows down to it and worships. He prays to it and says, 'Save me! You are my god!' They know nothing, they understand nothing; their eyes are plastered over so they cannot see, and their minds closed so they cannot understand.

How can we explain such folly? Only by realizing that idolatry is more than falling down before a piece of wood. As Paul states in his first letter to the Corinthians, concerning sacrifices made to idols, "The sacrifices of pagans are offered to demons, not to God, and I do not want you to be participants with demons" (1 Corinthians 10:20).

In some strange way, the act of deifying an inanimate object somehow allows that object to become the instrument of demons. Jeremiah 10:5 makes it clear that the idol itself is harmless: "Like a scarecrow in a melon patch, their idols cannot speak; they must be carried because they cannot walk. Do not fear them; they can do no harm nor can they do any good."

But when a man or woman falls down and worships it, the demon is given a foothold into his or her spirit.

Second, *occult practices.* The Old Testament is clear with respect to all forms of occultism.

> When you enter the land the LORD your God is giving you, do not learn to imitate the detestable ways of the na-

tions there. Let no one be found among you who sacrifices his son or daughter in the fire, who practices divination or sorcery, interprets omens, engages in witchcraft, or casts spells, or who is a medium or spiritist or who consults the dead. Anyone who does these things is detestable to the LORD; because of these same detestable practices the LORD your God will drive out those nations before you. You must be blameless before the LORD your God (Deuteronomy 18:9-13).

Unclean spirits have succeeded in creating a fascination with the occult that is as varied as man's imagination. In every society when men and women turn away from the true God, the diversity of occult practices becomes astounding beyond belief. However varied occult practices might be, they have one thing in common. They are open doors to demonic control.

> *Unclean spirits have succeeded in creating a fascination with the occult*

An incident from our experience in France illustrates this truth. After a weekend retreat at our ministry center, one of the young men failed to return home. Days later his body was found, washed ashore from the river into which he had thrown himself. Afterward we learned that he had been participating in occult practices in the home of a defrocked priest. A young lady who was a part of that group later told me that something bad had happened to all the young people who participated in those activities, and that three had taken their lives.

Too many of us have had to preside over the funerals of suicide victims whose descent into despair began with what seemed to be a harmless fascination with occult practices. Many of these practices are popularized by games, children's literature, and seemingly innocent movies that depict sorcery. No matter how apparently harmless such activities may appear on the surface, they have the potential of opening doors that could lead to demonic influence. God's severe warning in Deuteronomy 18 is just as applicable to us today as it was to the children of Israel centuries ago.

Third, *illicit sex*. Though there are no *direct* Scriptural references explicitly relating demonic activity to illicit sexual practices, both biblical and secular history contain an immense wealth of evidence for their association. Nearly every form of idolatry and satanic worship is associated with sexual practices, usually of the most degrading nature. That fact certainly sheds light on the extremely strict boundaries that the Scriptures place on sexual practices, as well as the strict prohibition given to the children of Israel concerning sexual union with the pagan populations.

Ancient secular writings tell us that the first act of the Sumerian kings was to have intercourse with Ishtar through her temple prostitutes, at which time they received supernatural powers. The worship of a mother goddess, associated with temple prostitution, continued through many civilizations, with such goddesses as Aphrodite, Cybele, Isis, Venus, and others.

Satanic worship often entails nudity as well as all kinds of perverted sexuality. There can be little doubt that the sexual revolution that has occurred in the last fifty years has been accompanied by a proliferation of demonic and satanic activity, much of it undetected by people whose worldview excludes the reality of the spirit world.

## The coming of hope

We must now make a huge leap from Satan's rebellion to the coming of the One who is humanity's unique hope, the Lord Jesus Christ. By the time our Lord appeared on the scene "in the fullness of the time" (Galatians 4:4, KJV), Satan had seemingly succeeded in bringing much of the earth under his perverted domination. Could he know, however, that his throne was not secure? He doubtless continued to be haunted by the words God had pronounced to him immediately after man's fall: "I will put enmity between you and the woman, and between your offspring and hers; he will crush your head, and you will strike his heel" (Genesis 3:15).

God's plan for Satan's defeat was the most closely-guarded secret of all the ages. It was only when God chose to reveal His mysteries that mankind began to learn about "God's secret wisdom, a wisdom that has been hidden and that God destined for our glory before time began. None of the rulers of this age understood it, for if they had, they would not have crucified the Lord of glory" (1 Corinthians 2:7-8).

In the next chapter we will begin to look at those mysteries.

## Discussion questions:

How does the existence of spiritual evil help explain the severity of God's judgments?

Why do we believe that there is no redemption for fallen angels?

What are Satan's three main tactics and how are they still being used today?

# Chapter Five

# A Mysterious Birth

*In spite of the devastation of civilization under the rule of Satan, a line of hope flows through the Old Testament, beginning with the promise of Genesis 3:15. It continues through the covenant promises to Abraham, and then focuses on the promise of the coming Messiah who would rule from the throne of David. This promise was fulfilled in the fullness of time with the miraculous conception and mysterious birth of the child of Bethlehem, when the eternal Son of God took on human form.*

IN SPITE OF THE SEEMINGLY ENDLESS CYCLE OF MAN'S rebellion and God's judgment in the Old Testament, there are glimmers of hope. Throughout its pages there is a promise of one who would come and establish justice, gaining back what Adam had so pathetically lost.

We have already looked at the first statement of this promise, spoken at the very beginning of man's history. In the mysterious words of Genesis 3:15, God announced that the seed of the woman would crush Satan's head.

Centuries later a man named Abram, later called Abraham, responded to the call of God and learned that he would be the father of a chosen nation whose descendants would be as innumerable as the grains of sand. Through him all the peoples of the earth would be blessed (Genesis 12:1-3). The promise was reiterated many times both to Abraham and to his descendants. In the New Testament we learn that those promises would be fulfilled in Abraham's seed, Christ. "The promises were spoken to Abraham and to his seed. The Scripture does not say 'and to seeds,' meaning many people, but 'and to your seed,' meaning one person, who is Christ" (Galatians 3:16).

## A coming Messiah

We read in the Old Testament that a descendant of David would later rule over a kingdom that would be universal and endless.

> *A descendant of David was to rule over a universal kingdom*

Romans 15:12, referring to Isaiah 11:10, states that the root of Jesse (the father of David) would rule over the nations. This is a prophecy of God's anointed one, the Messiah, by whom God's kingdom is to be established in Israel and in the world.

The Old Testament is replete with prophecies about the coming of this Messiah. The sheer number of those passages leaves absolutely no doubt that someday God's anointed one will rule over an eternal kingdom. Yet all of those passages are purposefully ambiguous with respect to their details. Even the prophets themselves did not understand fully the exact meaning of their messages, especially since some of the passages reveal that the Messiah would also know suffering (e.g. Isaiah 53).

> Concerning this salvation, the prophets, who spoke of the grace that was to come to you, *searched intently and with the greatest care*, trying to find out the time and circumstances to which the Spirit of Christ in them was pointing when he predicted the sufferings of the Messiah and the glories that would follow. It was revealed to them that they were not

serving themselves but you, when they spoke of the things that have now been told you by those who have preached the gospel to you by the Holy Spirit sent from heaven (1 Peter 1:10-12, emphasis added).

Peter goes on to say that even the angels desired to look into those things. Among those angels, there is no doubt that the one who was most concerned was the highest of all, Satan himself.

Satan, however, was very likely convinced that his position was secure. He could think of no way that God could depose him without denying either His righteousness or His love, which would result in the loss of the entire human race, and perhaps ultimately God's very throne.

In light of all this, tension in the unseen world soared when news began to circulate that a mysterious event had occurred in Nazareth. A virgin pledged to be married became pregnant under unexplainable circumstances, strangely reminiscent of Isaiah's prophecy in chapter 7, verse 14, which states that a virgin would conceive and bring forth a son. His name would be called Immanuel, meaning "God with us." This prophecy in Isaiah was followed by another in chapter 9. There the words are startling.

> *Tension in the unseen world soared*

For to us a child is born, to us a son is given, and the government will be on his shoulders. And he will be called Wonderful Counselor, Mighty God, Everlasting Father, Prince of Peace. Of the increase of his government and peace there will be no end. He will reign on David's throne and over his kingdom, establishing and upholding it with justice and righteousness from that time on and forever. The zeal of the LORD Almighty will accomplish this (Isaiah 9:6-7).

At the time that the prophecy of Isaiah 7:14 was given, no one except God Himself could have known its implications. Looking at it from a purely human standpoint, Isaiah's contemporaries would simply conclude that the term virgin referred to a young lady who had not previously had relations with a man, and that the birth of the child would be a normal birth. Further, the name Immanuel was one that was given by parents in honor of the God who is with us, rather than as a sign of deity.

> *Mary would become pregnant by the Spirit of God*

When the prophecy is seen in the context of Gabriel's announcement to Mary (Luke 1:26-38), however, it explodes with meaning. Mary would become pregnant not by a man, but by the Spirit of God. The name Immanuel would not be merely a title of honor but a designation of divinity. Jesus would fully be both God and man, as Paul so eloquently describes later in Philippians 2:5-11, saying that Jesus was in His very *nature* God, but that He took the *nature* of a servant, *appearing* as a man.

Was Satan made aware of the exact words pronounced by Gabriel in his appearances to Mary and later to Joseph? We cannot know. Is it possible that God surrounded those encounters by an impenetrable ring of angels, keeping this promise hidden from the evil prince of this world?

## The babe in Bethlehem

But whether or not he was fully aware of the circumstances of our Lord's conception, Satan was shocked into reality when suddenly a great angel appeared to a group of lowly shepherds on the hillsides outside of Bethlehem with an incredible announcement: "Do not be afraid. I bring you good news of great joy that will be for all the people. Today in the town of David a Savior has been born to you; he is Christ the Lord" (Luke 2:10-11). This could be none other than the announcement of the prophesied one, the Messiah, God's anointed one.

Immediately there appeared a vast host of angelic beings, perhaps the greatest assembly of angels in one place since God had assembled His angels to witness the creation. Usually we assume they were assembled merely to announce the coming of Christ to the shepherds, but that hardly explains their sheer numbers. They were doubtless sent to protect the newborn babe, and their protection probably continued throughout His earthly life. We can only imagine the intense struggles between the angels and the demonic forces focused on this tiny life, first as a fetus in His mother's body, then as a newborn in the stable. While myriads of angels announced His birth, myriads of demonic beings very likely shuddered in the shadows.

Satan was prepared for drastic action when, some time after the birth of Christ, the Magi from Persia arrived at the palace of Herod, saying, "Where is the one who has been born king of the Jews? We saw his star in the east and have come to worship him" (Matthew 2:2). Satan found a ready instrument for his response, the wicked Herod the Great, king of Judea.

Herod was a monster. Extremely jealous, he killed his favorite wife and two of her sons, even ordering the execution of another son when Herod himself was on his deathbed. History quotes Caesar Augustus as saying that it was better to be Herod's pig than his son.

There can be little doubt that Herod, one of the most evil of rulers, was subject to demonic influence and that the arrival of the Magi was soon common knowledge among the evil spirits of the unseen world. Though Satan could not know at that time that the Messiah was God in human form, he knew enough to realize that this babe in Bethlehem must be destroyed. Therefore, when the Magi failed to return to Herod, Satan incited Herod to order the massacre of all male children two years and under.

But it was too late. When the Magi left, an angel of the Lord appeared to Joseph in a dream. "'Get up,' he said, 'take the child and his mother and escape to Egypt. Stay there until I tell you, for Herod is going to search for the child to kill him'" (Matthew 2:13). Without delay they arose and left for Egypt during the night, staying there until news came of Herod's death.

## The necessity of the virgin birth

The incarnation—the eternal Son of God becoming an authentic human being—totally shatters our imagination. The human mind is incapable of grasping the enormity of the Creator coming to this tiny earth in bodily form by incarnating Himself in flesh and blood. Few believers seem to realize that God became a man not for a short period of years on this earth, but for all time. The resurrection gave Him a glorified body, but it was still the body of a man. This is clearly seen in Paul's words, written after our Lord's resurrection, where He is still called the *man* Christ Jesus (1 Timothy 2:5). At the very end of the Bible, Jesus still identifies Himself as the Root and Offspring of David (Revelation 22:16).

> *The incarnation totally shatters our imagination*

Yet though the virgin birth defies our imagination, without it Satan's defeat and our redemption would have been an impossibility. Of the billions of human beings born since God created the first man and woman, only one was worthy of opposing the dark prince of this world and gaining back what Adam had so tragically lost. Only by being born of a virgin could the man Jesus escape the contamination of Adam's sin, for the sin that entered the world by one man was passed on to all men (Romans 5:12). Through the virgin birth Jesus the man was born without the taint of the sinful nature.

## The childhood of Jesus

After Jesus returned to Nazareth we have few details concerning His life. He "grew and became strong; he was filled with wisdom, and the grace of God was on him" (Luke 2:40). The only event recorded in detail was when, at twelve years of age, He stayed behind in Jerusalem after Mary and Joseph had departed with the other pilgrims. Jesus had remained in the temple, reasoning with the doctors of the law. When His parents found Him, His answer to their concerns is significant: "'Why were you searching for me?' he asked. 'Didn't you know I had to be in my Father's house?'" (Luke 2:49).

Some see in this statement an expression of His self-consciousness of deity. For me that is doubtful. By the age of twelve there is no doubt that Jesus knew He was different from everyone else, and He most certainly had a growing sense of His messianic mission. But understanding that He was the Messiah is one thing; for Him to know that He was the eternal Creator who had come in the flesh is not something He would have deduced from His human reasoning. Jesus' complete consciousness of His divinity could come only through divine revelation (Matthew 16:17), as we shall see in the next chapter.

As far as we know, Jesus had a life that was uneventful from a human standpoint, working with His father in the carpenter's shop until He was about thirty years of age. Though we can imagine that Jesus' life was surrounded by intense angelic activity, the ordinary nature of His life had to be disarming to Satan, who saw Him less and less as a threat to his throne.

All this would change suddenly when Jesus was immersed into the waters of the Jordan River by His cousin John.

### Discussion questions:

Why was it impossible for the prophets themselves to know the full import of their prophecies?

Why was the virgin birth a necessity in the unfolding drama of redemption?

How much did Jesus really know about His identity during His childhood?

# Chapter Six

# The Fateful Encounter

*At His baptism the man Jesus became fully aware of His identity as the Son of God. He was driven by the Spirit into the desert for forty days, and in His weakened state He was confronted by Satan. During this temptation, the fate of the entire earth and its inhabitants rested on the shoulders of the man Christ Jesus. The object of the temptation was to push Jesus beyond His humanity and for Him to react as God, thus ending all hope of the redemption of mankind, as well as the hope of a man again becoming Earth's prince.*

THE NEW TESTAMENT IS A BOOK OF UNVEILING—THE unveiling of mysteries. In the language of the New Testament a mystery is not something difficult to understand, but a reality previously kept secret that is finally revealed. The announcement of the angels on the hills of Bethlehem signaled the beginning of the revelation of the divine secrets—secrets intently guarded since the beginning of creation. The meanings of the prophecies, ambiguous not only to their readers but to the prophets themselves, would now begin to be revealed. Underlying those prophecies was God's hidden plan, a plan so extraordinary that no human, angelic, or demonic intelligence was capable of unraveling it.

The one from whom these secrets were the most carefully guarded was of course Satan himself, along with his horde of evil subjects. Satan had no way of knowing that as he pursued his strategy against Christ, he was in reality simply playing into the hands of God and that every one of his malicious acts would turn against him with a vengeance.

> *Jesus completely emptied Himself of the independent exercise of His divine attributes*

Yet far more amazingly, *it is possible* that the full import of some of these secrets were veiled even from the knowledge of Jesus Himself *during* His earthly existence. How can we make such a statement? Because when the eternal Son entered the world as a fetus He completely emptied Himself of the *independent* exercise of His divine attributes. For instance, He did not know the time of His future return back to the earth, for in Mark 13:32 we read, "No one knows about that day or hour, not even the angels in heaven, nor the Son, but only the Father." Until His death and resurrection, whatever He did of a supernatural nature during His earthly existence was done through the Holy Spirit, who came upon Him in the form of a dove at the time of His baptism.

Many believers who are well-versed in the Scriptures seemingly do not have as much of a problem with the deity of Christ as they do in accepting His humanity and its implications. Although Jesus did not lay aside His deity in becoming a man, He lived and acted as a fully authentic human being with all its limitations. His was a life of total obedience to His heavenly Father; He spent vast amounts of time in prayer. "Although he was a son, he learned obedience from what he suffered" (Hebrews 5:8). The apostle Paul makes this very clear in his definitive statement on the incarnation in Philippians 2:5-11. Jesus Christ, who is by nature fully God, allowed Himself to become fully man. Though He remained fully God in *essence,* He allowed Himself to be limited to His humanity in *expression.* He took "the very nature of a servant, being made in human likeness. And being found in appearance as a man, he humbled himself and became obedient to death, even death on the cross" (vv. 7-8).

It was only after Jesus died, was raised from the grave, and ascended to heaven to sit at the right hand of the Father that God began to reveal to the world His carefully-guarded secrets. God's principal human instrument for

> *Jesus came to fulfill all righteousness*

their revelation was a man who, in his ignorance, had bitterly opposed God's plan. That man was totally transformed on the road to Damascus by his encounter with the very one whose memory he was attempting to obliterate, Jesus Himself. Paul makes it clear that the message he was announcing did not come from other men, but from the Lord. He was caught up into paradise to receive inexpressible revelations so great that to keep Paul from becoming conceited, God allowed him to be afflicted with a thorn of suffering—which he amazingly called *a messenger of Satan* (2 Corinthians 12:1-10).

Paul leaves no question about his divine commission:

> I have become [the church's] servant by the commission God gave me to present to you the word of God in its fullness—the mystery that has been kept hidden for ages and generations, but is now disclosed to the saints. To them God has chosen to make known among the Gentiles the glorious riches of this mystery, which is Christ in you, the hope of glory (Colossians 1:25-27).

## *The baptism of Jesus*

All this provides some background for the first momentous encounter of the incarnate Jesus with Satan. When Jesus was about thirty years of age He left His father's carpenter shop to go into the desert of Judea where His cousin John the Baptist was preaching his message of repentance and baptizing Jews in the Jordan River. John was the last of the Old Testament prophets; his mission was to announce the coming of the Messiah and the Kingdom of God. Jesus said of John, "Among those born of women there has not risen anyone greater than John the Baptist" (Matthew 11:11). John was a voice of one calling in the desert to prepare the way for the Lord: to "make straight in the wilderness a highway for our God" (Isaiah 40:3).

Although these two men had encountered each other when they were yet fetuses in the bodies of their respective mothers, a meeting that caused John to leap for joy in the womb of Elizabeth, we have no record of their having met since then. Imagine, therefore, John's emotion when he was approached by the very man whose mission he was to announce. *This was the Messiah!* This was the moment of destiny. What would be the Messiah's first act? Would He assemble all the people, march to Jerusalem, seat Himself upon a throne, and begin the conquest against His enemies?

Try then to imagine the confusion in John's soul when the Messiah asked the unthinkable—to be baptized along with all the repentant sinners massed around them. This was not the way a king is supposed to begin his reign. A king is supposed to sit on a throne and rule. Instead, Jesus joined the ranks of the subjects. John would never recover from the shock. Later he would send his disciples to Jesus to ask, "Are you the one who is to come, or should we expect someone else?" (Matthew 11:3).

For many, the baptism of Jesus is one of the enigmas of the Gospels. John's baptism was a baptism of repentance, yet we know that Jesus had nothing to repent about. Rather than try to explain all the theological implications, however, it is preferable simply to allow ourselves to be satisfied with Jesus' words. When John protested that he needed to be baptized by Jesus and not the contrary, Jesus said, "Let it be so now; it is proper for us to do this to fulfill all righteousness" (Matthew 3:15). Jesus' baptism is related to the totality of His identification with mankind. He would have to fulfill His role as the son of man before fulfilling it as the Son of God.

Hebrews 2:17 helps explain: "He had to be made like his brothers in every way, in order that he might become a merciful and faithful high priest in service to God, and that he might make atonement for the sins of the people."

## *The voice from heaven*

An understanding of the significance of the temptation begins with what happened at Jesus' baptism. It was at that time that Jesus received the revelation from heaven of His divinity. As Jesus came up out of the water, God the Holy Spirit descended upon him like a dove, and a voice from heaven proclaimed: "This is my Son, whom I love; with him I am well pleased" (Matthew 3:17). This is the first recorded account in the earthly life of Jesus that He was given divine revelation of His identity and was made fully conscious of His deity.

> *Jesus learns His true identity*

Today when we say that we are sons of God, we are referring to something entirely different from that heavenly announcement. We are saying either that we are God's sons by creation or God's sons by the new birth. The very context of this announcement from heaven, however, shows that it was nothing less than an affirmation of the deity of our Lord, the unique Son of God, one in nature with the Father.

It seems unthinkable for most people that Jesus could have already spent thirty years of His life without knowing that He was God in the flesh. They would point to His encounter with the doctors of the law at the age of twelve, thinking that encounter is proof that Jesus knew already that He was divine.

Yet, though the encounter at the temple certainly indicates that Jesus was conscious of His mission as the *Messiah,* it is no indication that He knew He was God. The expectation of the Messiah in no way implied that the Messiah would be God in the flesh.

For a fully authentic man to know that He was God the Creator—that is enormous. Jesus would not have known His identity while a fetus in the body of His mother. Further, it would be fanciful to assume that as a child He was aware of His divinity, in spite of the apocryphal stories of His performing miracles while growing up. And it seems unlikely that He had this God-consciousness even as a man in His father's carpenter shop.

Something had to happen at some point between His birth and the beginning of His ministry to make Him aware that He was God. When we fully understand the profound implications of Jesus' humanity, it is unthinkable that such knowledge could have originated from His human reasoning powers. We must always remember that our Lord had emptied Himself of having independent recourse to His deity.

Jesus' awareness of His true identity could have occurred only through a direct revelation from His heavenly Father. Compare Matthew 16:17, where Jesus acknowledges that Peter's confession of the Lord's deity was possible only because it was revealed to him by the Father in Heaven. If such a revelation occurred before the time of His baptism, we have no record of it. As commentator J. R. Dummelow states,

> If we take the most natural and obvious interpretation of the incident, we shall hold that our Lord's baptism marked the point in His career when there first awoke in Him the complete consciousness of His divine sonship, and of all the tremendous consequences which this unique relationship to God and man involved (*A Commentary on the Holy Bible,* Macmillan).

If that is true, the effect upon the man Jesus would have been cataclysmic. Under no circumstances could He have remained in the company of others. Led by the Spirit into the desert, He doubtless ran breathlessly back and forth among the foreboding cliffs and wild animals, trying to process this shocking disclosure, eating and drinking nothing for forty days.

*It was then, in Jesus' weakened state, that the reigning prince of this world confronted his Creator in the most insidious encounter since the Garden of Eden.*

## The temptation of Jesus (Matthew 4:1-11, Mark 1:12-13, Luke 4:1-13)
Many pass over the story of the temptation with little thought or comment. Yet it is one of the great pivotal events in the ultimate de-

feat of Satan. When Jesus faced Satan on the mount of temptation, the fate of the entire human race and perhaps even the throne of God weighed upon His shoulders. Why was the temptation of Jesus such a crisis event in the unfolding drama of man's redemption from the bondage of Satan? The answer to that question is one of the principal themes that runs throughout this book. It is because redemption required that Jesus gain back *as a man* what Adam had lost.

> **Satan is defeated by the man Christ Jesus**

The endless discussions concerning whether or not Jesus could sin miss the main thrust of this temptation. *The thrust of the temptation was not for Jesus to sin as we know sin, but to fail in His divine mission—by setting aside His humanity and independently manifesting His divine power and authority. To do so would mean that Jesus would fail in His mission.*

Satan's strategy was *to push Jesus beyond His humanity*, to cause Him to resort to His divinity. That being the case, the entire force of the first two temptations was contained in one tiny word: *if.* "*If* you are the son of God, prove it."

You can almost hear the mocking words of the tempter. "You … God? Is that what you think you heard when you were being baptized? You mean you think that God *really* said that? That is ridiculous. You are a man; can't you understand that? You mean you think you are my Creator? Come on, let's come back to reality and show some sense. You need to check your hearing. Something got garbled.

"Of course, if you want to *prove* that you heard right, there is a very simple way to do it. Why stay hungry if you are God? *If* you are the Son of God, nothing would be easier than to change one stone into bread. If you can do *that*, maybe even I will believe in you."

We have no idea what could have happened if Jesus had turned one stone into bread. Perhaps the world would have disintegrated at that very instant. We can be sure that we would not be talking about it now. God's unfolding drama of redemption would have ended in eternal disaster. Why? Because there was but *one* Son of God. When you accept the implications of the incarnation, you realize that Jesus could become man only *once*. He was the *last* Adam. *There would be no second chance.*

Jesus, proving His total obedience as a man, makes no attempt to argue with His tempter. He simply appeals to God's revelation, saying, "It is written, 'Man does not live on bread alone, but on every word that comes from the mouth of God'" (Matthew 4:4).

Satan, accepting defeat on his first try, changes his tactic and transports Jesus to Jerusalem, to the highest point of the temple. "I have enough sense to know that you will be beginning a mission to try to convince the people that you are their Messiah. Let's be realistic, though. You didn't make much of an impression on them when you allowed yourself to be baptized, did you? Don't make a fool of yourself. Here's your chance. Just jump off this pinnacle. I know Scripture as well as you, and it says, 'He will command his angels concerning you . . . so that you will not strike your foot against a stone' (Psalm 91:11-12). See the crowd down there? When they see this, to a man they will line up with you, and the rest will be easy."

Again Jesus refuses to give dignity to His tempter by entering into discussion. He says simply, "It is also written: 'Do not put the Lord your God [referring to the heavenly Father] to the test'" (Matthew 4:7). In perfect submission to the Lord His God, Jesus does not violate His humanity.

In the third temptation (following Matthew's order), Satan puts everything on the table. Taking Jesus to a high mountain, he shows Him all the kingdoms of this world. Luke's account of Satan's words is stunning. Speaking of the kingdoms of the world, Satan says, "I will give you all their *authority* and splendor, for *it has been given to me* [*by God Himself*], and I can give it to anyone I want to. So if you worship me, it will all be yours" (Luke 4:6-7, emphasis added).

If anyone has any question about Satan's being prince of this world by usurping the authority given to Adam, this statement ought to clear away all doubts. Satan claims authority over the kingdoms of the world. He states that the authority had been given to him. Since only God can give that kind of authority, it can refer only to Satan's becoming prince of this world at Adam's fall. He also says that he can give it to whomever he pleases. Jesus does not contest his statement.

Whatever else was in the warped mind of the tempter, one thing is certain. Satan was presenting to Jesus something that had the appearance of a legal transaction.

"Why go through the struggle, Jesus? Everything you want is now in my hands. Just sign on the dotted line and it will be all yours. What could be simpler? Bow down and recognize me as the prince of this world, and I'll pass the title on to you. How can I give it to you until you recognize that I have it? Just go ahead and get down on your knees. Nothing could be easier. Then everything will be over."

Again, the answer of our Lord was direct and final. "It is written, 'Worship the Lord your God and serve him only'" (Luke 4:8).

The first Adam had lost everything by affirming his independence toward God. The last Adam had just triumphed by affirming His submission to the Father. In His first personal encounter with the archenemy, Jesus as a man gained back the *right* to rule. Satan, defeated, left in shame. The angels came and attended our Lord in His weakened condition. His steps would now lead to the cross and ultimately to the final defeat of this unspeakably evil being.

## Discussion questions:

Why is it seemingly more difficult to accept the humanity of Jesus than His divinity?

Why do we distinguish between Jesus' consciousness of His being Messiah, and His consciousness of being God?

What was the essence of the temptation, and what can we learn from Jesus' reaction to Satan?

# Chapter Seven

# All-Out Warfare

*After Satan failed in tempting the last Adam to submit to his authority, he knew that he had but one recourse: to orchestrate the death of Jesus. Although Jesus' words concerning a resurrection had to strike fear into his mind, Satan had no other option but to seek to kill Jesus and imprison His spirit in Hades. Hades was the prison place of the spirits of the dead, over which Satan exercised authority as prince of this world. Satan failed to kill Jesus prematurely in the garden, where Jesus accepted the cup of man's sin, but he succeeded in scheming Christ's death on the cross. In doing so he played into God's hands and sealed his own doom.*

IMMEDIATELY AFTER HIS TRIUMPH OVER SATAN AT THE temptation, Jesus embarked on His public ministry. Matthew tells us that from that time on He began to preach repentance, saying that the kingdom of heaven was at hand. According to Luke's gospel, "Jesus returned to Galilee in the power of the Spirit" (Luke 4:14). Although Jesus would fulfill His earthly ministry within the limits of His humanity, this ministry would be characterized by extraordinary manifestations of divine power accomplished through the Holy Spirit.

Throughout the Old Testament Satan operated largely as the unseen prince, even while dominating man's history. When we come to the New Testament, this changes. Jesus' manifestations of supernatural power brought Satan out of the shadows. Satan and his evil angels could no longer hide. When we open the pages of the Gospels, we are immediately surprised by the widespread manifestations of demonic activity. Much of the people's suffering, whether physical or mental, is now revealed to have been spirit-induced. The New Testament, which covers a relatively short period of time, refers to Satan by name 35 times, "the devil" 33 times, and to demons more than sixty times.

Some of the encounters of Jesus with demonic powers are dramatic, such as the deliverance of a demonized man in the region of the Gerasenes. In his pitiful condition he was living among the tombs, naked and impossible to restrain even with chains. When he saw Jesus he cried out, "What do you want with me, Jesus, Son of the Most High God? I beg you, don't torture me!" (Luke 8:28). This man, unbelievably, was demonized not with one evil spirit, but a multitude, so many in fact that when Jesus cast them into the herd of swine on the hillside, two thousand swine (Mark 5:13) ran down the steep embankment and drowned in the lake.

The most fascinating aspect of this story is how the demons responded to Jesus. "They begged [Jesus] repeatedly not to order them to go into the Abyss" (Luke 8:31) in order to torture them *before the appointed time* (Matthew 8:29). Though it is impossible to fully know the import of these statements, it seems evident that by this time the demons were aware of the fate that awaited them if their master failed in his attempt to overcome the Lord. Further, it also seems evident that many demons had already been consigned to the abyss through the ministry of Jesus and His disciples.

### Satan's last resort

Jesus' encounters with the demons were only a prelude to what was to come, however. The situation faced by their dark prince had become sinister. By this time we can only imagine that Satan was thoroughly perplexed by this Jesus of Nazareth. Though Satan was well aware of the heavenly announcement of Jesus' divinity, he doubtless remained mystified by all its implications. Let's keep reminding ourselves that the divine secrets concerning God's drama of redemption were still meticulously guarded, even from the angels.

Therefore, after failing to prevail over Jesus at the temptation, Satan was left with but one option—to seek to put Jesus to death. He had to realize that his strategy was fraught with risk. He was doubtless increasingly haunted by the thought that he could indeed be playing into the hands of God. His evil subordinates had reported to him that Jesus was openly speaking of His death, and, horror of horrors, of a resurrection. If Satan succeeded in killing Jesus, would He stay dead?

This idea might shed some light on Jesus' exclamation when Peter rebuked Him for speaking of His death. Jesus responded in the strongest terms possible: "Get behind me, Satan! You are a stumbling block to me; you do not have in mind the things of God, but the things of men" (Matthew 16:23). Was Satan using Peter to attempt to gain more information? The menace of resurrection had apparently thrown Satan into confusion and fear.

> *Satan was left with but one option— to seek to put Jesus to death*

In spite of all this, Satan knew that orchestrating the death of Jesus was his only resort. After all, he still held dominion over Hades, called Sheol in the Old Testament. Hades should not be confused with eternal hell, called Gahenna in the New Testament. Hades was the prison house of the spirits of the dead, and because it was a part of the world system, Satan was still its legitimate prince. Throughout human history we have record of only one person escaping Hades before the resurrection of Christ. It was Moses, who was released in order to appear with Elijah at the transfiguration. Elijah did not die; he had been taken directly into heaven (2 Kings 2:11). According to Jude 9, Moses' release from Hades provoked a violent dispute between the devil and Michael the archangel. Though Satan had no direct power over the souls in Hades, the Jude passage certainly indicates that this dreadful place was under his authority.

On the night of Jesus' last meal with His disciples, after He had stated clearly that one of the disciples would betray Him, Satan entered into Judas. Though accounts indicate that *demonic* possession was widespread during Jesus' ministry, we have only two instances of *satanic* possession in the Scriptures: that of Judas and that of the coming antichrist. The task was too great to be assigned to one of his subordinates; Satan himself would control the mind and heart of his chosen instrument to bring Jesus to His death. Immediately after his possession by Satan, Judas disappeared into the darkness.

> *The agony of eternity's supreme act of love and sacrifice began in the Garden of Gethsemane*

At that last supper Jesus took a towel, washed the feet of the disciples, then offered them the symbols of His body and blood, soon to be shed for them. He proceeded to share with them some of His most intimate conversations yet. He told them He must soon leave them, but that they would not be orphans, for His Spirit would come, not just to be with them but in some mysterious way to live in them. After singing a hymn, they descended from the city, crossed the Kidron brook, and went to Gethsemane, the place where Jesus often retreated for prayer.

### The agony of the garden

Just as legions of angels had congregated outside Bethlehem to sing the praises of the birth of the Lord, legions of fallen angels must have congregated at Gethsemane to orchestrate His betrayal and ultimate condemnation and death at Jerusalem. Otherwise how can we explain that within a few short days many who welcomed Jesus into the city as their Messiah would turn upon Him and demand His death?

The agony of eternity's supreme act of love and sacrifice began in the Garden of Gethsemane, a place once so comforting but now foreboding beyond description. For Jesus, the agony he experienced during the immediate hours following His arrival were infinitely beyond human comprehension. The very language used to describe His suffering was strained to the limit. Never before or since has any human being suffered such torment. The sweat falling from His brow was like drops of blood.

> "Abba, Father," he cried, "everything is possible for you. Take this cup from me. Yet not what I will, but what you will" (Mark 14:36).

> *The dreaded cup was the sin of mankind and its wages, total separation from the Father*

What was this cup from which Jesus recoiled with such torture? Most commentators refer to it as merely the suffering He was experiencing, without explaining further. Some even refer to it as His approaching death, and seem to emphasize that Jesus' torment was provoked by His human fear of death. Yet Jesus had plainly announced to His disciples that He must be killed and that He would rise again (Matthew 16:21).

The cup from which Jesus so desperately recoiled was nothing other than the cup of mankind's sin and its wages, total separation from His Father. "God made him who had no sin to be sin for us, so that in him we might become the righteousness of God" (2 Corinthians 5:21). God the Son, who throughout eternity knew nothing but purity, holiness, and righteousness, now faced the utmost horror of drinking to the very dregs the abominations of all mankind when the sins of all men would be placed on Him at the cross.

This horrendous prospect filled Him with inexpressible revulsion, to the point that He feared immediate and premature death, as is evident in His anguished cry, "My soul is overwhelmed with sorrow to the point of death" (Matthew 26:38). Yet He knew He must not lose consciousness; He must stay alive in order to drink the cup fully and bear the sin and guilt of all men.

The garden scene gives meaning to the otherwise baffling words in Hebrews 5:7-8:

> During the days of Jesus' life on earth, he offered up prayers and petitions with fervent cries and tears to the one who could save him from death, and he was heard because of his reverent submission.

Was Jesus praying in the garden to be delivered from the death on the cross? Not at all.

Jesus had talked freely of His death. Jesus was instead praying for deliverance from a *premature* death apart from the cross, a death that would compromise His eternal mission. Jesus' agony in the garden was so intense that He despaired of His life. He knew that to atone for our sins, He would have to give Himself willingly. This premature death was being orchestrated by Satan himself, though Satan could not have known all the implications of what was happening.

All through this horrific experience, the most horrendous drama of all time, the disciples slept. This is incredible beyond belief. How could they be so totally insensitive to the anguish of their Master? Even when Jesus awakened them for what must now follow—the betrayal, the trial, and the crucifixion—they were still unaware of the reality of the drama that was being played out before their eyes.

The events that followed brought Jesus' passion to its dreadful climax. In the light of burning torches Judas led his unholy band to the place where he knew he would find his Lord. Trembling with emotion, he approached his Master and betrayed Him with a kiss. A brief struggle ensued in which the impulsive Peter cut off the ear of the servant of the high priest. "'Put your sword back in its place,' Jesus said to him, 'for all who draw the sword will die by the sword'" (Matthew 26:52). Soon the disciples fled into the darkness. Before the night was over Judas would be hanging from a tree. Peter, the same Peter who had confessed Jesus as the Son of God, would be weeping bitterly because of his inconceivable denial of his Lord.

Jesus was taken to Jerusalem to appear before the high priest. After being scourged and humiliated by the soldiers, He was brought before the Jewish council in a mock trial and condemned to death. Pilate, the Roman governor, sought to free Him, but the fury of the Jewish leaders against Jesus was so great that he yielded to their pressure. Jesus was led to the place of the skull and hanged on the cross.

Darkness fell upon the earth. Before gasping His final breath, Jesus cried out, "My God, my God, why have you forsaken me?" What is the meaning of those dreadful words? Where was the spirit of Jesus during the three days that His body lay in the tomb?

That will be the subject of the next chapter.

## Discussion questions:

Why, in spite of the risk, did Satan have no other recourse than to put Jesus to death?

Why was Jesus' suffering in the garden so intense?

How was Jesus' prayer to be delivered from death answered (Hebrews 5:7)?

# Chapter Eight

# Satan Dethroned

*The sin of mankind, requiring the chastisement of the righteous Father, was laid upon Jesus. The righteousness of Jesus, the object of the Father's love, was imputed to all who would put their trust in Him. The Father could now freely express His love to His creatures without violating His righteousness. Before dying physically Jesus suffered spiritual death—the outer darkness of separation from the Father. Victory, however, was achieved when the spirit of Jesus descended into Hades. Kicking open the door of that dreadful place from the inside, He led the saints, from Adam to the thief on the cross, into the very presence of God. Satan and his evil angels were led in infamy to be stripped of their authority before a watching universe. Jesus' body was raised from the dead and He was crowned in the heavenly places in full glory and honor as the rightful Prince of the world.*

ON THE HILLTOP OF OUR ETERNAL DESTINY STANDS THE cross. The cross is the focal point of all history. There is only one Son of God. He became a man only one time. He had but one chance to triumph over His temptation by mankind's archenemy, Satan. He could die only once. The cross was the culmination of all God's dealings with mankind from the moment of Adam's rebellion against his Creator. And since then, everything flows from the cross.

The physical agony suffered by our Savior on the cross defies comprehension. Without doubt, crucifixion is one of the most agonizing forms of capital punishment ever invented by man's cruelty. Death was not induced by the painful injuries inflicted on the wrists and legs, but by asphyxiation. Hanging there between heaven and earth, his arms outstretched in an abnormal position and his head bursting with pain, the victim of crucifixion would find it impossible to breathe unless he attempted to push himself up by his weakened legs, only to collapse again into a state of suffocation. Depending upon the physical fortitude of those being crucified, this ghastly process could go on for hours, and in some cases even for days, until as an act of mercy the victim's legs were broken, rendering him unable to avoid suffocation, thus releasing his soul into eternity.

But the Jesus hanging on the cross was no ordinary victim. He was the eternal Son of God. His capacity for suffering was infinite.

The words of an old Negro spiritual doubtless ring in our ears: "Were you there when they crucified my Lord?" What believer has not tried to imagine being there, witnessing the agony of the garden and the betrayal, being shocked by the mock trials and call for Jesus' death, being sickened by the terrible scourging and agonizing walk up to Golgotha, being horrified by the blood-curdling cry of Jesus: "My God, my God, why have you forsaken me?"

Yet even had we been there, witnessing all these events, our understanding of the cross would still be woefully incomplete. The greater significance of the cross lies in what was going on *beyond* the veil of the visible in that mysterious domain that remains imperceptible to human eyes. To attempt even a tiny understanding of the staggering cost of our redemption, we must descend much farther beneath the cross of Jesus than those who were standing there as witnesses of His crucifixion. We must descend into the realm of the unseen.

## Jesus in outer darkness

Few words are more heart-rending than those of the prophet Isaiah: "He was pierced for our transgressions, he was crushed for our iniquities" (Isaiah 53:5). When our Lord had drunk the cup of our iniquities to their last dregs, He cried out, "My God, my God, why have you forsaken me?" (Matthew 27:46).

*Jesus' desperate cry on the cross tells us that at that instant the eternal unity between the Father and Son was shattered. Before experiencing physical death, Jesus experienced separation from the Father. This could mean nothing less than spiritual death, for spiritual death is separation from God.*

The spiritual implications of this separation are unthinkable. When His eternal union with the Father was shattered, in a real way Jesus suffered eternal hell for us, even while He was alive physically. Whether it was for a split second or for the entire three hours of darkness on the earth matters little. *He was the eternal One.* Because His capacity to suffer was infinite, He brought eternity into that instant of time.

The language of the Bible concerning eternal hell is very vivid. No amount of imagination will allow us to comprehend the agonizing realities of hell, any more than we can know the blessedness of heaven. The image that seems to convey the *essence* of eternal hell more than any other is that of outer darkness, which can only mean isolation. Jude, as well as Peter, speaking of godless men, states that "blackest darkness" is reserved for them forever (Jude 13, 2 Peter 2:17). Hell is the outer darkness of total separation from God.

Total isolation means the loss of all identity. Relationship with others is a basic need not only of humanity, but of divinity, as we see in the interrelationship of Father, Son, and Holy Spirit. Total solitary confinement is an unbearable form of punishment. Even secular writers understand that. The French atheistic philosopher Jean-Paul

> *When His eternal union with the Father was shattered, Jesus suffered eternal hell for us*

Sartre wrote *No Exit,* a play in which he depicted hell as a comfortable living room where people would have to experience eternity in the presence of the people they found intolerable. At a certain point in the play a door opens and everyone jumps up and runs for the open door. Then they stop, turn around, and slowly return to the living room and take their seats. Beyond that open door was what Sartre called *néant*—or nothingness. It is ironic that an atheist, apparently ignorant of biblical truth, could so graphically portray the outer darkness of total isolation, eternal separation from God.

Therefore, though the physical suffering of Jesus on the cross was ghastly beyond description, it pales in comparison to His separation from the Father. That the love of our eternal God is so enormous that He would be willing to endure this kind of anguish and distress completely shatters our whole being—body, soul, and spirit.

Yet, there was no other course possible. The sin of mankind had to be laid upon Him. No one else in heaven, or earth, or below the earth, could take *His* place. Only He could do it, and He could only do it alone. "He was cut off from the land of the living; for the transgression of my people he was stricken. . . It was the LORD's will to crush him and cause him to suffer" (Isaiah 53:8, 10).

How can we restrain ourselves from falling upon our faces before Him? Forever we will cry out, "Worthy is the Lamb, who was slain, to receive power and wealth and wisdom and strength and honor and glory and praise!" (Revelation 5:12).

### *Our sins nailed to the cross*

In Colossians 2:13-14 we read,

> When you were dead in your sins and in the uncircumcision of your sinful nature, God made you alive with Christ. He forgave us all our sins, having canceled the written code, with its regulations, that was against us and that stood opposed to us; he took it away, nailing it to the cross.

When criminals were crucified, their crimes were often written down and nailed to their cross. According to the various translations of this passage it would appear that a heavenly record exists of everyone's transgressions against the ordinances of God. That record includes future transgressions as well as past. Those transgressions were taken off our account and nailed to the cross, being laid on Christ.

During the ages before Jesus died, the sins of believers were covered over by the blood of sacrifices sprinkled on the mercy seat in, first, the tabernacle, then the temple. This covering, however, was only temporary. As the writer of the letter to the Hebrews states, "It is impossible for the blood of bulls and goats to take away sins" (Hebrews 10:4). The death of Christ brought eternal pardon to saints who died before Christ. The apostle Paul writes:

> God presented [Christ] as a sacrifice of atonement, through faith in his blood. He did this to demonstrate his justice, *because in his forbearance he had left the sins committed beforehand unpunished*—he did it to demonstrate his justice at the present time, so as to be just and the one who justifies those who have faith in Jesus (Romans 3:25-26, emphasis added).

For those of us who live some twenty centuries after those words were written, they seem almost commonplace, especially if we have heard the gospel for years. Yet the implications of the apostle's statement are incredible beyond imagination. *The death of Christ means that we are free*—free from the authority of sin and death. The ceaseless accusations of the devil have no more foundation, even though he might continue to accuse.

## Jesus' descent into Hades

The Apostles Creed says that at His death, Christ descended into *hell*. For ages this phrase has created confusion in the minds of Christians. We have just seen that the eternal hell Jesus suffered was the outer darkness of His separation from the Father. This was suffered while He was still alive physically, as is evident from His statement on the cross, "My God, my God why have you forsaken me?" (Matthew 27:46, Mark 15:34).

It was His *spiritual* death that atoned for our sins. Jesus stated, *before dying physically*, "It is finished" (John 19:30), indicating that the cost of redemption had been paid. The unspeakable separation

73

from the Father had been accomplished. The thick curtain hiding the holy place of the temple was torn from top to bottom, showing that the Father had accepted Jesus' sacrifice.

Then Jesus cried out with a loud voice, "Father, into your hands I commit my spirit" (Luke 23:46). When He had said this, He breathed his last. "With that, he bowed his head and gave up his spirit" ( John 19:30). It was then that His spirit departed from His body and He experienced physical death.

> *Jesus' spirit descended into Hades, the prison place of the spirits of the dead*

It was therefore at the instant of His physical death that the spirit of our Lord descended into what the Apostles Creed calls *hell.* However, the term translated *hell* in the original Greek version of the Creed is not *Gehenna,* the term for eternal hell, but *underworld,* which is another term for Hades or Sheol, the prison place of the spirits of the dead.

The spirit of Jesus did not descend into *hell* to suffer the chastisement of His Father. This chastisement had already been suffered in His spiritual separation from the Father, the object of His eternal love. When the spirit of Jesus descended into Hades, He had already triumphed over the illegitimate prince of darkness. Though not yet crowned, Jesus descended into Hades in triumph, as the new Prince of this world.

Because Hades was a part of the world system of which Satan was then still the legitimate prince, it was under his authority. That truth is doubtless what gives meaning to Hebrews 2:14, where we read that the devil held the "power [meaning dominion] of death." Though the Bible does not specifically say that Satan held the keys of Hades before the death of Christ, this statement certainly implies it. Satan did not have the authority to *inflict* death without God's permission, but he held dominion over the spirits of the dead once they were in his prison house. Of course, that is no longer the case, for our risen Lord now holds the keys of death and Hades (Revelation 1:18).

What we know about the descent of Jesus into Hades is based on two New Testament passages. Ephesians 4:9 says that Jesus descended into the "lower, earthly regions," or more literally, to the "lower parts of the earth." Some argue that this text merely refers to the incarnation and would identify "lower, earthly regions" simply as the earth. However, the original text plainly says that He descended not simply *to* the earth, but into the "*lower parts*" of the earth. This certainly refers to something different from the physical earth; which is why most commentators refer to it as Hades. The term "lower, earthly regions" corresponds to the "underworld" in the Apostles Creed.

The second passage is 1 Peter 3:18-20: "He was put to death in the body but made alive by the Spirit, through whom also he went and preached to the spirits in prison who disobeyed long ago when God waited patiently in the days of Noah while the ark was being built."

As the prison house of the spirits of the dead, Hades held captive the spirits both of the saved and the unsaved dead. In the story of the rich man and Lazarus (Luke 16:19-31) we learn that the rich man was in torment, whereas Lazarus was in a state of blessedness in the presence of Abraham. There was a great gulf between the two so that no one could cross from one side to the other. However, both men were in Hades.

## Satan's humiliation

We can only imagine the horrid shrieks of pleasure from the demonic powers surrounding the great Prince of Darkness when Jesus cried out on the cross, "It is finished" and experienced physical death. Satan no doubt was brandishing his keys to Hades and awaiting with hideous anticipation the arrival of his archenemy. His last resort was to seek to imprison the spirit of Jesus in this dreadful place where he was the master.

The fiendish viciousness of Satan and the demonic powers was short-lived. Although the spirit of Jesus descended into Hades,

Hades now had no power to imprison Him. The awful price of redemption had been paid. Nor could Hades continue to imprison those whose sins had been covered through the forbearance of God (Romans 3:25). In an incredible display of power, Jesus kicked open the gates of Hades from the inside. In triumphal procession Jesus led the army of the Old Testament saints into the very presence of God, from Adam to the thief on the cross to whom Jesus had promised, "Today you will be with me in paradise."

> *Satan, the legal prince of this world, was stripped of his authority*

This triumphal procession involved far more than just the saints. The words of Colossians 2:15 jump off the page at us: "Having disarmed the powers and authorities, he made a public spectacle of them, triumphing over them by the cross." Satan, the legal prince of this world, was stripped of his authority. Just as defeated military chiefs are humiliated by marching in shame in the military processions of the victors, Satan and his angels were forced to follow the saints into the presence of God to be humiliated before the watching universe, including the multitude of the saved whom he had held captive century after century.

The dark prince had now been dethroned, stripped of his keys and authority. His legitimacy as the prince of this world was now a thing of the past. The world now has a new Prince! Though many centuries would pass before the new Prince would be publicly crowned before the watching universe, God had already

> exalted him to the highest place and [given] him the name that is above every name, that at the name of Jesus every knee should bow in heaven and on earth and under the earth, and every tongue confess that Jesus Christ is Lord, to the glory of God the Father (Philippians 2:9-11).

From now on the prince of darkness knows that his cause is lost. His insignia of rank was torn off his shoulders and his sword is broken.

He is now no more than a vandal—the most powerful vandal in the universe, to be sure, but a vandal and a squatter, seeking incessantly to destroy what God is doing, and squatting on the inheritance of God's children.

That does not mean that he will be immediately consigned to the Abyss or thrown in the lake of fire. In the pages that follow we will see him again and again, feverishly exerting his fiendish power.

But a new era in the unfolding drama of redemption had begun. From that time on all who die in Christ will go, not to the prison place of the dead, but into the very presence of God. The apostle Paul awaited with anticipation being away from the body and at home with the Lord (2 Corinthians 5:8). And when Stephen, the first martyr, was stoned, he "looked *up to heaven* and saw … Jesus standing," awaiting his coming. "Lord Jesus, receive my spirit," he cried out (Acts 7:55-59, emphasis added).

> *The resurrection of Christ represents the most staggering show of power ever displayed*

### Resurrection

On the first day of the week the stone was rolled away from the tomb in the garden. Jesus' spirit, after leading the triumphal procession to paradise, had returned to claim His body. The disciples of Jesus found only the grave clothes. Angels proclaimed His resurrection. His disciples would now be transformed from fearful fugitives into the apostles of a new age.

The resurrection of Christ represents the most staggering show of power ever displayed in the universe. In Paul's account of the resurrection, he virtually empties the Greek language of its terms for power.

> [This] *incomparably great power* … is like the *working of his mighty strength* which he exerted in Christ when he raised

him from the dead and seated him at his right hand in the heavenly realms, far above all rule and authority, power and dominion, and every title that can be given, not only in the present age but also in the one to come (Ephesians 1:19-21, emphasis added).

In this passage the apostle Paul makes it clear that we should not think of this display of resurrection power as being limited only to what happened when the body of Jesus left the tomb. Resurrection began when the spirit of our Lord descended into the prison place of the dead, confronting the prince of darkness face to face. It continued when He opened the gates of Hades, leading the spirits of the saved to paradise and humiliating Satan and his angels by stripping them of their authority. It reached its culmination when His spirit was reunited with His body and He was seated in power and authority at the right hand of the Father, above all other authorities for all time.

The resurrection of Jesus Christ puts to rest forever any doubts that we might have concerning our own resurrection. Romans 4:25: "He was delivered over to death for our sins and was raised to life for our justification." Just as the appearance of the high priest's leaving the Holy of Holies in the Old Testament ritual was proof that God had accepted the sacrifice, so the appearance of our Lord is eternal proof that God has accepted the supreme offering for sin, and has declared us righteous. But even before the trumpet sounds and our own bodies rise from their graves, those of us who are born and adopted into the family of God have already been raised and seated with Christ in the heavenly places with respect to our legal position. The resurrection of our Lord marks the beginning of an entirely new creation—a new race whose citizenship is in heaven. To Him be glory throughout all ages!

## Discussion questions:

What is the difference between hell and Hades?

On what basis can we state that Jesus suffered eternal hell on the cross?

If Satan has been stripped of his legitimacy, how can he still exercise power?

# Chapter Nine

# A New Creation

*The resurrection marks the start of a new race of people whose citizenship is in heaven. Their authority supersedes that of Satan and all his angels, whose former authority is now totally illegitimate. The believer's position is in Christ, raised with Christ, and seated in heavenly places far above all other powers. This is a legal transaction, giving the believer divine authority. In addition, Christ is in the believer, filling him or her with power, and transforming the believer into His image.*

THE DEATH AND RESURRECTION OF JESUS CHRIST REPRESENT more than a new chapter in the drama of redemption; they initiated a cosmic revolution. The world now has a new prince; Jesus is seated at the right hand of the Father and is crowned Lord of all lords. Satan, after exercising authority for thousands of years as the prince of the kingdoms of this world, has been dethroned and publicly humiliated, along with his vast army of unclean spirits. The souls of those whose sins are covered have been delivered from the prison of the dead and led in glory into paradise.

But there is far more. The resurrection of Jesus Christ and His subsequent coming at Pentecost in the person of the Holy Spirit have resulted in a new creation. Paul makes this clear in 2 Corinthians 5:17:

"If anyone is in Christ, he is a new creation." The believer is not just a changed person; he is a new creation. The old order of things, which began with Adam, is now effectively set aside. The new has come.

God's beautiful creation at the beginning of history was fatally flawed only days after Adam and Eve were placed in the Garden of Eden. Sin and death penetrated every facet of humanity. The resurrection of Jesus, however, began the process of making all things new. Believers born again by God's Spirit are adopted into His family as His eternal children, with all the rights and privileges that such a relationship entails.

*All this is nothing less than the beginning of an entirely new race of people.*

The apostle Peter puts it like this:

> You are a chosen people, a royal priesthood, a holy nation, a people belonging to God, that you may declare the praises of him who called you out of darkness into his wonderful light. Once you were not a people, but now you are the people of God; once you had not received mercy, but now you have received mercy (1 Peter 2:9-10).

## We have been raised with Christ

We saw earlier that in Paul's great prayer in Ephesians 1 he asks that the eyes of our heart might be enlightened, so that we might not only know the hope of our calling and the glorious riches of our inheritance, but also God's incomparably great power toward us. This is the power which God exerted in Christ in raising Him from the dead and seating Him at His right hand (vv. 18-20).

In light of those words, the statement of the apostle Paul in Ephesians 2:6 is absolutely astounding. Many believers simply pass over it, because it seems to defy comprehension.

Paul states, "God raised us up with Christ and seated us with him in the heavenly realms in Christ Jesus." What can that mean? Since Paul is writing to people whose feet were firmly planted upon this earth, his words certainly do not refer to their physical resurrection and ascension; their physical resurrection is yet future. Yet those words must be taken at face value. And if we take them seriously, what do they mean?

There is only one possible conclusion. Those words refer to our judicial status, our legal position. We are no longer citizens of this earth; our citizenship is in heaven (Philippians 3:20). If we were given a divine passport, our address would not be the place of our present residence. It would be "in Christ, right hand of God, heavenly realms." Though we continue to be residents of this world, we are aliens and strangers (1 Peter 2:11), for legally we are "citizens with God's people and members of God's household" (Ephesians 2:19). If we are still residents of this world, it is because we have been sent here as ambassadors, with a mission of announcing the message of reconciliation (2 Corinthians 5:20).

> *We are no longer citizens of this earth; our citizenship is in heaven*

The implications of the previous paragraphs relate to every aspect of our relationship with the Lord and our conflict with the forces of evil. Look again at the words of the first two chapters of Ephesians. Take time to reflect upon those realities until they penetrate deeply into your soul.

First, *Christ has been raised and seated at the right hand of God in the heavenly places, "far above all rule and authority, power and dominion, and every title that can be given, not only in the present age but also in the one to come"* (Ephesians 1:21, emphasis added).

Second, *"God raised us up with Christ and seated us with him in the heavenly realms in Christ Jesus"* (Ephesians 2:6, emphasis added).

In conclusion, *every believer is seated with Christ "far above all rule and authority, power and dominion, and every title that can be given, not only in the present age but also in the one to come"* (Ephesians 1:21, emphasis added).

If you have the faith to believe and personalize these spiritual realities, you can begin to understand why, throughout this book, we have emphasized this astonishing truth—that we who are "in Christ" outrank Satan and all his angels. The most humble believer who has been redeemed from this world has authority that is superior to the most exalted of all angelic beings. To resist Satan in the name of Jesus means that he has no other recourse than to flee from us (James 4:7).

Those of us who are members of this new race are intimately identified with the eternal prince, Christ.

We are "*in Christ.*" That clothes us with divine *authority.*

Christ is "*in us.*" That fills us with divine *power.*

## Every believer is in Christ

The New Testament is replete with the expression "in Christ." At times it is simply used to designate those who have placed their faith in the Lord. In numerous instances, however, it is used as a term related to our legal identity, referring to our judicial position as members of a new race of people. This is the meaning of Paul's statement in 2 Corinthians 5:17, "if anyone is *in Christ,* he is a new creation" (emphasis added).

> *Satan no longer has any basis for his accusations*

The implications of our being in Christ are far-reaching. To be *in Christ* means of course to be justified—declared righteous in the sight of God. Satan no longer has any basis for his accusations. Justification does not imply that God is unaware of our sins and shortcomings. It means that He sees us as covered with the righteousness of Christ. Just as our sins were laid upon Christ, His righteousness was laid upon us.

To be *in Christ* means not only to be justified. It also means that we have been legally adopted into the Lord's family. Ephesians 1:5 says that God "predestined us to be adopted as his sons through Jesus Christ, in accordance with his pleasure and will."

In Christ, therefore, we have been given an entirely new identity. Paul says in Galatians 4:6-7 that we have received the full rights of sons. According to the Roman law of adoption, which was a legal process, the adopted child was entitled to the father's name, possessions, and family sacred rights. The adopted son became an heir, even when formerly he might have been a slave. He was given a share of the inheritance.

All of that means that Satan no longer has any *right* to be squatting on our inheritance. We have been given authority over the devil and all his evil angels. Through prayer and affirming our position in Christ, we can resist him, forcing him to flee. We no longer have to see ourselves as helpless victims who are condemned to constant failure. "Thanks be to God, who always leads us as captives in triumphal procession in Christ and through us spreads everywhere the fragrance of the knowledge of him" (2 Corinthians 2:14).

## Christ is in every believer

When Jesus told His disciples of His departure during His last evening with them, they were filled with grief. "I will not leave you as orphans," He said, "I will come to you" (John 14:18). That promise was fulfilled on the day of Pentecost when Jesus, through His Spirit, personally embodied the life of every believer.

When the apostle Paul writes about this truth, he calls it "the mystery that has been kept hidden for ages and generations, but is now disclosed to the Lord's saints." Then he states, "To them God has chosen to make known among the Gentiles *the glorious riches* of this mystery, which is Christ in you, *the hope of glory*" (Colossians 1:26-27, emphasis added). In Colossians 2:9-10 he exclaims, "For in Christ all the fullness of the Deity lives in bodily form, and *you have been given fullness in Christ*, who is the head over every power and authority" (emphasis added). Paul's words mean that the temple of God's pres-

> *Every believer has now become the temple of God*

ence was no longer an edifice in Jerusalem with its Holy of Holies. Every believer has become God's temple through the Lord's Spirit with all that this implies, both individually for each Christian, and collectively for the church.

To grasp this truth we need to remember that the Holy of Holies in the temple at Jerusalem was so sacred that entrance was denied to all except the high priest, who entered once a year with the blood of the covenant. Tradition says that ropes were attached to his legs so that he could be pulled out if stricken by God. But wonder of wonders, God's temple would now be His people. "God's temple is sacred, and you are that temple" (1 Corinthians 3:17).

The implications of Christ's being in us are just as vast as the implications of our being *in Christ*. Let us meditate on just three of them.

First, *because Christ is in us, we are given divine power*. Without that power we would be helpless in standing against the schemes of the devil and his cohort of evil spirits. It is no surprise that in Paul's three great prayers in Ephesians and Colossians, he petitions the Lord that believers might experience this supernatural power. Paul states that the same power that raised Christ from the dead is now made available to every Christian (Ephesians 1:19-20). He prays that "out of his glorious riches he may strengthen [them] with power through his Spirit in [their] inner being" (Ephesians 3:16). He asks that they might be "strengthened with all power according to his glorious might so that [they] may have great endurance and patience" (Colossians 1:11).

Second, *because Christ is in us, we are being transformed into His image*. This means that we are being sanctified—being *made* righteous by His transforming presence. No passage presents this truth more powerfully than 2 Corinthians 3:17-18: "Now the Lord is the Spirit, and where the Spirit of the Lord is, there is freedom. And we, who with unveiled faces all reflect the Lord's glory, are being transformed into his likeness with ever-increasing glory, which comes from the Lord, who is the Spirit." The presence of Christ in us results in our being *transformed*, which literally means *metamorphosed*.

Sanctification does not come from morbid introspection. In fact, introspection can become one of the wiles of the evil one, causing us to focus on ourselves and our failures rather than on our identity in Christ. Further, sanctification does not result from a legalistic attitude toward the law. The law is good, but it is not an end in itself. It is an expression of the will of the Lord. The law, however, has no power to change us, only to condemn us when we fail. Our Lord seeks inner transformation, not outer conformity.

Third, *because Christ is in us, we are able to bear fruit.* One of the most beautiful images of our relationship with the Lord is in John 15:1-17 where Jesus compares Himself to the vine and the believer to the branches. The purpose of the vine is to bear fruit. That is possible only when the branch is firmly grafted into the vine, allowing the life of the vine to flow into the branch. This image makes it clear that the branch is incapable of bearing fruit on its own; it must be vitally connected to the vine. Our relationship with Christ is not merely truth to be understood; it is truth to be lived by intentionally abiding in the Lord Jesus.

> *Our relationship with Christ is not merely truth to be understood; it is truth to be lived*

Two of the aspirations of committed believers are intimacy with the Lord and a sense of purpose or significance. These aspirations can be fulfilled only when we intentionally respond to the risen Christ in us, by seeking His power through prayer, by reflecting His image through worship, and by bearing fruit through abiding in Him.

A new Prince has assumed power and authority. The forces of darkness have been thrown into consternation. One day the new Prince will return in the greatest display of power ever seen. Until then, however, He has done the unthinkable. *He has made the hearts of His chosen servants His throne.*

## Discussion questions:

In what way is the believer a member of a new race?

What does Paul mean when he says that we have been raised with Christ?

Explain the implications both of the believer being in Christ and of Christ being in the believer.

# Chapter Ten

# Spiritual Vandalism

*Although Satan has been stripped of all legitimacy, God allows him to continue to exercise great power and deception. Why does God allow that? Because those who enter the spiritual kingdom must do so through personal choice. The full expression of man's love for God can be shown only when freedom of choice is possible. Satan's chief weapons are the world, the flesh, and the powers of darkness.*

AT THE CROSS SATAN LOST HIS LEGITIMACY AS PRINCE OF this world, but he continues to exercise his fiendish influence. The disarming of Satan in Colossians 2:15 must be understood as the loss of his authority, not his power. Though the term *power* is used in some translations of the Bible to translate *authority*, these terms refer to two different realities. Power is the *ability* to impose force upon others; authority is the *right* to do so. Just as it is possible to have authority without power, it is possible to exercise power without authority.

An unarmed officer standing in the middle of the street directing traffic has the authority to stop drivers. If, however, a driver refuses to recognize his authority, the officer is powerless. On the other hand, a group of protesters have the power to block the road with their vehicles though they are given no authority to do so. As we have seen, believers are given both power and authority in their conflict with the enemy.

> *Satan operates no longer as a prince, but as a vandal and a squatter*

Because he has lost his legitimacy, Satan operates no longer as a prince, but as a vandal and a squatter. A vandal is someone who is bent on destruction. Often he destroys something he knows he will never obtain. A squatter is someone who occupies a property illegally. Squatters usually can be dislodged only by legal action.

Satan's tactics are diverse. He often operates openly, as a roaring lion looking for someone to devour (1 Peter 5:8). He also operates under cover as an angel of light (2 Corinthians 11:14). As a roaring lion he mercilessly brings people into bondage through drugs, illicit sex, unrestrained ambition, or open occultism. As an angel of light, he just as effectively makes people his slaves through sins that are considered insignificant or socially acceptable. Any willful disobedience toward our Lord may offer Satan a foothold.

Satan's evil influence is everywhere. As the ruler of the kingdom of darkness, his agents are spread throughout the earth, bringing entire territories and nations under his domination. If we had the ability to peer into the unseen world, we would probably be surprised to see how many of the political leaders of the world's kingdoms are being manipulated by unseen spiritual powers.

Though Satan knows that his doom is sealed and that his destiny is the lake of fire, he is intent on destroying everything God is doing. He has a scorched earth strategy among the nations, seeking to leave nothing good in this world for the Lord to find when He returns. As He approaches his impending doom, Satan's fury will continue to increase in intensity.

## Satan's schemes

Paul states in 2 Corinthians 2:11, "We are not unaware of his (Satan's) schemes." Satan's schemes against the Church are rooted in three realities. These realities underlie his entire strategy and form the base of his operation. They are the *world* (human society without God), the *flesh* (the sinful nature), and *the kingdom of the air* (evil spirits).

Paul alludes to all three of these realities in Ephesians 2:1-3 (emphasis added):

> As for you, you were dead in your transgressions and sins, in which you used to live when you followed the ways of *this world* and of the ruler of *the kingdom of the air*, the spirit who is now at work in those who are disobedient. All of us also lived among them at one time, gratifying the cravings of *our sinful nature* and following its desires and thoughts.

The three form an unholy team, each one playing off the others.

## Satan, god of this world

The Bible uses the term *world* in different ways. In the Old Testament the term usually refers to the *Earth*, the physical world that God created. In the New Testament most of the references to the world refer to the earth's *inhabitants*.

There is, however, a third meaning to the term, and it is always used in a negative sense. The same apostle who said, "God so loved the world" (John 3:16), also said, "Do not love the world or anything in the world. If anyone loves the world, the love of the Father is not in him" (1 John 2:15). It is obvious that the world God *loves* is not the same as the world we are *not to love*. God loves the world of people; we are not to fall in love with the world system.

In His prayer in John 17 Jesus used the term *world* with all three of its meanings. He said that the Father loved Him before the creation of the *world*, our planet (v. 24). He said that we are sent *into the world*, the world of people (v. 18). But He also said that we are not *of the world*, the present age (v. 16).

When the Bible uses the term "world" in a negative sense, it is referring to human society alienated from God's influence. The term "secular humanism" corresponds very closely to this use of the term. In humanism man thinks he is the master, but that is only an illusion. The tragedy of secular humanism is that man is duped by Satan into thinking that man is the master of his fate, whereas he is merely a puppet, being manipulated by unseen powers. What is thought to be total freedom from all restraint is in reality enslavement. Enslavement is in itself tragic, but slaves who are deceived into thinking they are free are all the more pitiful.

> *Worldliness*
> *is an*
> *inversion*
> *of values*

We are to refuse conformity to the world. The Greek text of Romans 12:2 identifies the world as "this age." For too long the church defined worldliness by a list of unacceptable practices. That is unfortunately still the case with many legalistic believers. By doing so, the church becomes an easy prey to worldliness, too often disguised by a spiritual veneer. Many churches find their members thoroughly impregnated with worldliness without recognizing it.

Why? Because worldliness is not defined by certain practices but by values. *Worldliness is an inversion of values.* The world is characterized by the substitution of man's values for those of our Maker. In the world's system man supplants God, the present overshadows eternity, self becomes more important than others, physical needs supplant spirituality, and man lives for power, pleasure, and possessions. The list goes on and on.

Human society has always glorified the world. In our western society this glorification reached its apex with the Enlightenment, which effectively attempted to put God on the shelf in every aspect of life. When the values of this world system penetrate the church, our love for God is effectively quenched. It happens no matter how hard we try to sanctify the values of the world system.

The world, or this present age, is one of the three powerful tools of Satan, the "god of this age," to lead all mankind astray (2 Corinthians 4:4). Though Satan is no longer the *legitimate* prince of this world, he has succeeded in making himself its god for many vast segments of the population. He has effectively clothed the values of humanism with a counterfeit spirituality, causing mankind to worship and serve created things rather than the Creator (Romans 1:25). When the possessions and practices of this world become the object of a person's devotion, Satan himself becomes his or her god.

The intimate relationship between Satan and the world is clearly seen in the passage from Ephesians 2 quoted previously. According to this passage, to follow the "ways of this world" is also to follow "the ruler of the kingdom of the air, the spirit who is at work in those who are disobedient." The world system is a tool of Satan to manipulate and enslave its inhabitants. Satan leads the whole world astray (Revelation 12:9).

## Satan, enticer of the flesh

Just as the term "world" has more than one meaning in the Bible, so does the term "flesh." Occasionally this term refers to all humanity, as in Genesis 6:12 where it indicates that "all flesh had corrupted his way upon the earth" (KJV). Usually, however, the term simply refers to the physical part of men and animals. But in the New Testament epistles, "flesh" often refers to the sinful nature, and is in fact translated as such in newer versions. The flesh is mankind's moral sickness which has resulted from man's separation from God, bringing disintegration into our very beings. The "flesh," or sinful nature, finds its seat in the subconscious—defined as that part of our spirit over which we have no im-

> *The flesh is the source of unlimited evil*

mediate conscious control. The subconscious is like a rubbish bin into which all our thoughts, experiences, and perceptions are thrown and jumbled together, detached from rational and moral categories.

The flesh is the source of unlimited evil. In Galatians 5:19-21 the apostle Paul gives us a depressing litany of the works of the flesh:

> The acts of the sinful nature are obvious: sexual immorality, impurity and debauchery; idolatry and witchcraft; hatred,

discord, jealousy, fits of rage, selfish ambition, dissensions, factions and envy; drunkenness, orgies, and the like. I warn you, as I did before, that those who live like this will not inherit the kingdom of God.

This list covers the entire range of evil: sexual passion, occult practices, egotism, division, lack of self restraint.

It is true that the devil gets blamed for many things that are incited purely from the sinful nature of man. "The devil made me do it" is too often a cop-out for unrestrained passion. James makes it clear that most sin comes directly from our depraved nature. "Each one is tempted when, by his own evil desire, he is dragged away and enticed. Then, after desire has conceived, it gives birth to sin; and sin, when it is full-grown, gives birth to death" (James 1:14-15).

Any one of those sinful practices can become addictive. Even apart from demonic influence, the flesh exercises profound power over the will and can be completely broken only by a firm decision to walk in the Spirit in order not to fulfill the lusts of the flesh.

But though the sinful nature can independently be the source of man's sins, it nevertheless remains one of Satan's three main entry points in his strategy against the church and her saints. As god of this world, he has easy access into the desires of the flesh, for the world provides the bait for stimulating the passions. The enticement of the world is the prelude to enticement by the sinful nature. John definitely connects the world and the flesh, showing that they work as a team: "For everything in the world, the lust of the flesh, and the lust of the eyes, and the pride of life, is not of the Father, but is of the world" (1 John 2:16, KJV).

## Satan's footholds

It is evident that any sinful practice can provide a foothold for Satan and become a means of spiritual bondage. That is made clear in Ephesians 4:26-27: "'In your anger do not sin': Do not let the sun go down while you are still angry, and do not give the devil a foothold."

The phrase "do not give the devil a foothold" simply means that we must not give him a place *within* our life. It is evident from this passage that sinful conduct provides an open door for spirit activity *within* a person's being. Though there is disagreement concerning whether Christians can be *possessed* by demons (the expression does not appear in the Scriptures), it is evident that when we allow sin to enter any of the rooms of our consciousness, we are opening the door for demonic influence and even control. Much of what is called depression by psychologists is spiritual oppression, leading to bondage. Spiritual bondage is far more prevalent than most would believe. Where there is bondage, freedom will not necessarily come from counseling or meditation. It will require affirming our position in Christ, repenting and renouncing sin, forgiving those who have sinned against us, and rebuking and resisting the devil.

> *To resist the devil is to affirm our position in Christ*

To resist the devil is to affirm our position in Christ and to order the devil and his angels to cease their evil influence in our lives. The devil can be resisted in simple and direct terms, or with great passion and eloquence. One of the most eloquent rebukes of Satan was written by Thomas à Kempis, the 13th-century monk:

Away, thou unclean Spirit! Blush, thou miserable wretch! Most unclean art thou that bringest such things unto mine ears. Begone from me, thou wicked Seducer! Thou shalt have no part in me, but Jesus shall be with me as a strong Warrior, and thou shalt stand confounded. I had rather die, and undergo any torment, than consent unto thee. Hold thy peace and be dumb; I will hear thee no more, though thou shouldest work in me many troubles (*The Imitation of Christ*, Book III, Chapter 6).

Fortunately, an increasing number of churches and counselors are becoming aware of the widespread influence of the spirit world in all facets of Christians' lives—spiritual, psychological, and physical. If the realities of the unseen world were revealed, we would be amazed at the pervasive activity of unclean spirits. And we would be equally amazed at the ministry of God's protecting angels, sent as messengers to His children through their prayers.

## Satan, ruler of the powers of darkness

When the Bible uses the terms "Satan" or "the devil," it is often referring to the vast network of evil beings that execute his schemes. This hierarchy of evil is frequently referred to in the epistles. The most complete reference is Ephesians 6:12 where we read that "our struggle is not against flesh and blood, but against the rulers, against the authorities, against the powers of this dark world and against the spiritual forces of evil in the heavenly realms." (We will comment on this passage in detail in chapter 12.) Satan is neither omnipresent nor omnipotent, but his emissaries have penetrated all aspects of society, provoking mankind to bow to their chief.

In Isaiah's taunt against the king of Babylon, he quotes Lucifer, the morning star, as saying, "I will make myself like the Most High" (Isaiah 14:14). From the Garden of Eden until the present, Satan is driven by one impassioned craving—to be worshiped. It is no mistake that he is called the *god* of this world. Throughout his monstrous career he has been relentless in seeking to turn men and women from their worship of the true God, and the substitutes he offers them are seemingly endless.

Satan succeeds brilliantly, for man is a religious being. Created in the image of God, he has what the philosopher Pascal called "a god-shaped void" in his inner being. He is made to worship, and if Satan succeeds in turning him away from the true God, he will fall down to worship anything.

As the god of this world, Satan has the ability to transform anything into a religious act, captivating the devotion of those who offer themselves to it. Disguising himself as an angel of light, he generally succeeds in concealing himself as the object of this devotion, except when he gains total mastery over his subjects and plunges them into occult practices. Only then does he begin to reveal his true identity, leading his worshipers to total submission.

The New Testament is replete with examples of how Satan and his angels intervene directly in the lives of unsuspecting believers.

He is able to remove the good seed sown by the Lord, and to replace it with bad. He inflicts sickness. He manipulated the disciples and filled the hearts of believers such as Ananias. He prevents believers from fulfilling their ministry. He sets traps for believers. And the list goes on. (See the list of references below.)

But though Satan and his angels wreak havoc everywhere, his main target is not the kingdom of this world. He is already effectively dominating it and its subjects through his illegitimate power. His main fury is being poured out on our Lord's spiritual kingdom, the church—the kingdom of those whose eyes have been opened, who have turned from darkness to light, and who have been delivered from the power of Satan to God (Acts 26:18).

In our next chapter we will discover how Satan was totally taken by surprise by a small group of believers gathered in an upper room in Jerusalem. An extraordinary new chapter had begun in the unfolding drama of redemption.

*A partial list of references indicating the awareness of the early church to the pervasive influence of unseen powers:*

Satan filled the heart of Ananias (Acts 5:3).

Some are under the power of the devil, are children of the devil, and fall under the same judgment as the devil (Acts 10:38, 13:10; 1 Timothy 3:6).

Unrepentant sinners were handed over to Satan (1 Corinthians 5:5, 1 Timothy 1:20).

Satan tempted believers (1 Corinthians 7:5).

Pagan sacrifices are offered to demons (1 Corinthians 10:20).

Satan can outwit believers (2 Corinthians 2:11).

Satan, the god of this world, can blind the minds of the unbelievers (2 Corinthians 4:4).

Satan can lead astray the mind of the believer (2 Corinthians 11:3).

Satan masquerades as an angel of light (2 Corinthians 11:14).

Satan tormented Paul with a thorn in the flesh (2 Corinthians 12:7).

The devil can gain a foothold in the believer's life (Ephesians 4:27).

We wrestle against the rulers, authorities, and powers of the world and the spiritual forces of evil (Ephesians 6:12).

Satan prevented Paul from going to Thessalonica (1 Thessalonians 2:18).

Satan will control the lawless one (2 Thessalonians 2:9).

We must be guarded from the evil one (2 Thessalonians 3:3).

Satan can trap church leaders (1 Timothy 3:7).

Some will follow doctrines of demons (1 Timothy 4:1).

Believers can turn away and follow Satan (1 Timothy 5:15).

Believers can fall into the devil's trap (2 Timothy 2:26).

Earthly wisdom is of the devil (James 3:15).

Believers must resist the devil (James 4:7).

As a roaring lion, Satan can devour the believer (1 Peter 5:8).

He who is sinful is of the devil (1 John 3:8).

Some are in the synagogue of Satan (Revelation 2:9, 3:9).

Idolaters worship demons (Revelation 9:20).

Demons perform miraculous signs (Revelation 16:14).


## Discussion questions:

Explain the difference between power and authority.

Why must we define the world in terms of values and not in terms of practices?

If Satan has been stripped of his authority, why is he still called the "god of this world"?

## Chapter Eleven

# God's Secret Weapon

*The death and resurrection of Christ began not only a new race, but also a new era. Rather than immediately inaugurating His physical reign, the newly crowned prince, in the person of His Spirit, incarnated Himself in a lowly group of believers called the church. The church, as the body of Christ, would be built by the Lord and would prevail against the forces of darkness. Whatever would be bound in the church would be loosed from the authority of Satan.*

IT IS FASCINATING TO TRY TO IMAGINE THE CONSTERNATION in the devil's camp after his humiliation and the crowning of the new prince, Jesus Christ. They had to be totally distraught by the sudden turn of events. Their cause was forever lost, and in their confusion and dread they awaited their fate with trepidation. What would be the first act of the newly crowned prince of this earth?

Once again the forces of darkness were taken completely by surprise. Rather than sending His heavenly army to bind them and throw them into the dreaded pit, our Lord sent His Spirit to dwell in a lowly cluster of men and women who were gathered in prayer in an obscure room in Jerusalem. It was the day of Pentecost, and His church was born—the church that was destined to become the instrument of His eternal plan to bring all things under the headship of the Lord.

Concerning the church, the words of the apostle Paul in Ephesians 3:10-12 are astounding. "His intent was that now, through the church, the manifold wisdom of God should be made known to the rulers and authorities in the heavenly realms, according to his eternal purpose which he accomplished in Christ Jesus our Lord." As the church has spread throughout the world, her presence has been a constant demonstration of the manifold wisdom of God and an evidence of Satan's ongoing condemnation. Every time someone is delivered from the powers of darkness, every time a new disciple is baptized into the church, every time a believer wins a victory over sin—the dark rulers and authorities in heavenly realms are filled with fury.

### A spiritual kingdom

When Jesus began His earthly ministry, He announced that the kingdom of God was at hand. On hearing this, His followers would not have known that the earthly kingdom predicted in the Old Testament would be preceded by a spiritual kingdom. The establishment of Christ's kingdom would be in two phases, just as was the coming of the King. When Jesus came the first time, He came as the Lamb who would suffer. When He returns, He will come as the Lion who will reign (Revelation 5:1-12).

> *The establishment of Christ's kingdom will be in two phases*

There is a touching scene in Revelation 5 that illustrates this truth. The apostle John was given a vision of God holding a scroll sealed with seven seals. Many believe that this scroll symbolizes the title deed to the earth. To break the seals and open the scroll was to assume ownership of the earth—ownership once given to Adam but then usurped by Satan. A mighty angel proclaimed in a loud voice, "Who is worthy to break the seals and open the scroll?" (v. 2). Tragically, no one in heaven or on earth or under the earth was found who could look inside the scroll or even open it.

The apostle wept uncontrollably because no one was found who was worthy. But then he heard a voice: "Do not weep! See, the Lion of the tribe of Judah, the Root of David, has triumphed. He is able to open the scroll and its seven seals" (v. 5).

When John turned to look, he was not prepared for what he saw. Instead of a *lion*, he saw a *lamb*. The elders sang a new song:

> You are worthy to take the scroll and to open its seals, because you were slain, and with your blood you purchased men for God from every tribe and language and people and nation. You have made them to be a kingdom and priests to serve our God, and they will reign on the earth (vv. 9-10).

The new prince will one day return to rule as a lion. But until then He is calling people to Himself, interceding for them before the throne, and preparing them to rule with Him. And He is doing this as the Lamb.

## The church—the spiritual kingdom

After His resurrection and His exaltation on His throne in heavenly places, far above all authorities and powers, our Lord began establishing His *spiritual* kingdom. This spiritual kingdom began on the day of Pentecost, when the believers were filled with the Spirit of the Lord and the church was born. Though the church is a spiritual kingdom, it is not the fulfillment of the kingdom promises of the Old Testament. They will be fulfilled in the millennial kingdom.

From Pentecost to the present, however, the Lord is rescuing believers from the dominion of darkness and bringing them "into the *kingdom* of the Son he loves" (Colossians 1:13). Then one day, at the appointed time, our Lord will descend from heaven in power to set up His *earthly* kingdom. "The kingdom of the world has become the kingdom of our Lord and of his Christ, and he will reign for ever and ever" (Revelation 11:15).

In God's marvelous drama of redemption, the church is therefore the spiritual kingdom by which the new Prince is gaining back what the first prince, Adam, had lost. It was by their personal choice that Adam and Eve had lost their freedom by disobeying their Creator. It is by personal choice that God's chosen ones have the privilege of entering the Lord's spiritual kingdom. Freedom of choice is possible, however, only when mankind has the option of choosing to follow the god of this world rather than submitting to the One who is now the rightful Prince. Without this option man would be little more than a spiritual marionette.

> *Satan unwittingly became God's tool for the redemption of those destined to reign*

God's gift of authentic freedom has been bitterly costly, but as C. S. Lewis states: "Of course God knew what would happen if they used their freedom the wrong way; apparently He thought it worth the risk" (*Mere Christianity*, Harper Collins 2001, page 48).

For redemption to be authentic, it is necessary to allow Satan, deprived of all legal rights but retaining all his power and deception, to move freely upon this earth. Yet, at the same time, the Spirit continues to call men and women to turn from darkness to light, from the power of Satan to God (Acts 26:18). God is patient, "not wanting anyone to perish, but everyone to come to repentance" (2 Peter 3:9).

All this offers an explanation for God's tolerance of the second prince, Satan, who is now without a throne but who seems to roam at will, looking for someone to devour (1 Peter 5:8). *Satan unwittingly became God's tool for the redemption of those destined to reign.* Those who choose to enter the kingdom are freed from their bondage to Satan.

### His glorious church
Matthew 16:18-20 records the announcement of the new spiritual kingdom.

> And I tell you that you are Peter, and on this rock I will build my church, and the gates of Hades will not overcome it. I will give you the keys of the kingdom of heaven; whatever you bind on earth will be bound in heaven, and whatever you loose on earth will be loosed in heaven.

Those words of Jesus in the Gospel of Matthew concerning the church have been subject to a great diversity of interpretations, some quite fanciful. Just as Satan and his angels were incapable of understanding their meaning, neither can we unless we interpret them in context. The church is one of the mysteries that God kept secret for millennia, only to be revealed fully after the death and resurrection of Jesus. Paul's words and letters, and in particular, the letter to the Ephesians, shed light on this passage.

Paul reveals the church as God's masterpiece. The purpose of human history is the calling out and perfecting of the Bride; she is the focal point of God's great plan. She is the means by which God reveals His manifold wisdom. She is the object of the Lord's eternal affection. She exists already in all her glory in the mind of Christ. One day she will be displayed in that glory before the watching universe.

None of the above was made known to the disciples when our Lord announced the church. But let us return to the words of Jesus to examine them more carefully.

**"I will build my *church*."** The church is *ekklesia,* an assembly of the called. This term was commonly used, both by the Jews and the Romans, to designate assemblies of people called together for a specific reason. Paul, however, infuses it with profound meaning. The church is the spiritual family of those who have been *called out* of the world and Satan's domination into a new life and relationship. Paul's mission in the world was given to him in these words: "to open their eyes and turn them from darkness to light, and from the power of Satan to God, so that they may receive forgiveness of sins and a place among those who are sanctified by faith in [Christ]" (Acts 26:18). The church is not an earthly kingdom; she is a body of men and women called out of this world system, given heavenly citizenship, and sent back into the world as the Lord's ambassadors.

**"I will build *my* church."** It is only as we read Paul's letters that we begin to fathom the depth of the intimacy between our Lord and His church. Paul calls the church a *body* in which the life of the members is dependent upon the head; she is not merely a collection of body parts. The church is a spiritual *building*, growing up into a temple, in which the Lord dwells through His Spirit; she is not simply a pile of stones. The church is a *bride*, the object of the eternal affection of the Lord, who is bringing her to perfection through His love; she is not a parenthesis in God's plan for the ages. The church is a *household*—she is a family of believers, each having an intimate relationship with the Lord; she is not primarily an institution.

> *The church is a spiritual incarnation of Jesus Christ*

Though it may sound incredible, the church as the body of Christ is in a real sense a second incarnation of Jesus Christ. Our Lord dwells in us through His Spirit. In His first incarnation Jesus *procured* our redemption; through His second incarnation, He *proclaims* this redemption.

**"The gates of Hades *will not prevail* against it."** Since in ancient cities the officials held court at the gates of the city, many commentators teach that the term *gates of Hades* refers to the principalities and powers of the unseen world. The church is given the power to prevail over those authorities. She is equipped with spiritual weapons of warfare that can prevail over all her enemies (Ephesians 6:10-18). The Spirit who is in us is greater than he who is in the world (1 John 4:4). That power enables the church to be a witness throughout the entire world, even in places where the strongholds of Satan are the most entrenched (Acts 1:8).

**"I will give you the *keys of the kingdom of heaven."*** A key is a symbol of authority. Jesus did not offer the disciples the keys *to* the kingdom of heaven; He alone possesses them. His offer concerns the keys *of* the kingdom of heaven. This is another way of saying that Jesus was conferring His authority upon the disciples, giving them the right to call people from the kingdom of darkness into the kingdom of light.

**"Whatever you *bind on earth* will be *bound in heaven*."** Many connect this to the power to bind unclean spirits in Jesus' name. The parallel passage in Matthew 18:15-20, however, would indicate that Jesus is referring to spiritual binding through submission to the authority structures of the church. Here the words of the Lord concerning binding and loosing are related to spiritual unity. In this passage Jesus states that if a brother or sister sins against us we are to seek reconciliation, either personally or with the help of others, or ultimately through the intervention of the church. Then He says,

> I tell you the truth, whatever you bind on earth will be bound in heaven, and whatever you loose on earth will be loosed in heaven. Again, I tell you that if two of you on earth agree about anything you ask for, it will be done for you by my Father in heaven. For where two or three come together in my name, there am I with them (Matthew 18:18-20).

*The words of the Lord concerning binding and loosing are related to spiritual unity*

To be bound in heaven is therefore to be bound by the spiritual protection of the church in our conflict with the forces of darkness. When we are in spiritual unity with our fellow believers, we are bound by the church's authority structures. On the other hand, as Paul indicates in 1 Corinthians 5:1-5, when believers are no longer under this protection, they are handed over to Satan. That means that they become vulnerable spiritually to Satan and his forces. These words have serious implications for all Christians. If we violate the spiritual authority of the church through disunity, we expose ourselves to the illegitimate authority of Satan.

God's will is to bind together all things in heaven and in earth, the invisible and the visible world, under the headship of our Lord Jesus Christ. His instrument for doing this is the church, the spiritual kingdom of our legitimate Prince.

> For he has made known to us in all wisdom and insight the mystery of his will, according to his purpose which he set forth in Christ as a plan for the fullness of time, to unite all things in him, things in heaven and things on earth (Ephesians 1:9-10, RSV).

The fullness of times began at Pentecost, when the church was born and became the fullness of Him who fills everything in every way (Ephesians 1:23).

*The church is God's secret weapon.* Never in all his scheming could Satan have unraveled God's strategy, that of calling out a people, filling them with His fullness, and using them to defeat Satan and his angels through love and not through force.

"To him be glory *in the church and in Christ Jesus* throughout all generations, for ever and ever" (Ephesians 3:21, emphasis added).

God's secret weapon is no longer secret.

## Discussion questions:

Why must the physical kingdom be preceded by a spiritual kingdom?

In what way is the church a spiritual kingdom?

What does it mean to be "bound" by the church?

# Chapter Twelve

# Spiritual Conflict

*After the church came into existence, she became the chief target of Satan's scheme, becoming the focus of spiritual opposition. However, every member of the church is legally seated in Christ at the right hand of God with the authority to resist Satan and his angels. To enable the church to stand against the schemes of the devil and his angels, God provides her with spiritual armor, equips her with the sword of the Spirit, and empowers her through prayer.*

FEW VERSES IN THE NEW TESTAMENT ARE MORE SOBERING for the Christian than Ephesians 6:12. Nowhere else do we have such a panorama of the vast array of evil forces in the hierarchy of Satan. The devil's entire army is displayed. Paul refers to *rulers*, to *powers*, to *world forces of darkness*, and to *spiritual forces of wickedness in heavenly places* (NASB). This passage depicts a power struggle of the most intense magnitude imaginable. As is true in Ephesians 1:19, where Paul seems to empty the Greek language of its terms for power with respect to God, so here he does so regarding the devil's power. Yet the power of God will prevail. Believers are exhorted to oppose the powers of evil by relying on the same power that God exerted in raising Christ from the dead. Just as Satan was defeated then, he can be defeated now.

This passage should certainly awaken us to the fact that unseen forces are real, and that they are a powerful force for evil in our lives. Paul's words should convince even the most skeptical. Too often we expend our energy in struggling against people rather than the real enemy.

> *The church is the prime target of Satan's fury*

To be sure, our awareness of the forces of evil must not blind us to the presence of the "horses and chariots" of the Lord (2 Kings 6:17)—the angels who are "ministering spirits sent to serve those who will inherit salvation" (Hebrews 1:14). The sheer number of ministering angels defies our imagination. If it is true that Satan brought a third of the angels under his authority by causing them to rebel against their Creator, we can assume that two-thirds of them remain faithful to the Lord. We can conclude that Satan's forces are outnumbered two to one!

In the home office of my mission organization we have a machete which was left years ago by one of the pioneer missionary women in Africa. Working alone, she went from village to village sharing the good news. In one particular village she was given a hut in which to spend the night. The next morning, after a good night of rest, she awakened to find the men of the village grouped together in consternation. "Who were those warriors surrounding your hut?" they shouted. "We were going to kill you during the night, but ran away when we saw them." The intrepid missionary thanked the Lord and requested their machete as a souvenir of the angelic intervention. Stories like that are too numerous to ignore.

### The church under attack

The church is the prime target of Satan's fury. That should not come as a surprise, for the church is the body of Christ, the spiritual incarnation of the Lord. If Satan hates our Lord, he hates the church with the same intensity. Though Satan succeeded in putting Jesus to death, the resurrection dashed his hopes for overturning the throne of God. He was outwitted by the hidden wisdom of God, and it is the church that continually displays this "manifold wisdom of God to the rulers and authorities in the heavenly realms" (Ephesians 3:10). Every victory of the saints drives the enemy to greater fury.

If we take seriously the Bible's predictions concerning the end times, we must conclude that Satan's war against the church will intensify as the coming of the Lord approaches and will end only when Jesus returns. Yet as many point out, too many churches have replaced their warfare mentality with a blueprint mentality; they seem to think that spiritual struggle has been eliminated because everything is mapped out in God's plan.

But though God's plan guarantees Satan's ultimate defeat, Ephesians 6:10-20 forcefully shows us that the war is real. In a war some battles are won and some are lost. Whenever the church seeks to overcome her invisible enemy through human force, power, or ingenuity, she faces potential defeat. On the other hand, whenever the church remembers that the weapons of our warfare are not of this world, she has the potential to abolish strongholds (2 Corinthians 10:4) and to walk in triumphal procession (2 Corinthians 2:14).

We who belong to Christ do not need to fear Satan's array of evil spirits. The Lord who is in us is greater than the one who is in the world (1 John 4:4). Christ's mission is to destroy the works of the devil (1 John 3:8). We are seated in Him "far above all rule and authority, power and dominion, and every title that can be given" (Ephesians 1:21). Though Satan is a roaring lion looking for someone to devour, when we resist him he has no recourse but to flee from us (1 Peter 5:8-9).

## The church's armor (Ephesians 6:13-18)

Though we need not fear, we do need to be prepared. Because of the intensity of the battle, the description of the church's armor in Ephesians 6 assumes enormous meaning for every believer. Paul begins this significant passage by exhorting us to be strong in the Lord and in the power of His might. Our struggle is not with a visible enemy, but with the invisible powers of darkness.

Clothing ourselves with the armor of God, we are to *stand*. Paul uses the word four times for emphasis. Jesus promised that the "gates of Hades," the invisible forces of evil, would not be able to prevail against His church (Matthew 16:18). The promise of victory does not mean, however, that we can allow ourselves to become passive. To stand is to aggressively resist the enemy. We must not let our guard down.

> ## We must be intentional in putting on the armor of God

We must therefore be *intentional* in putting on the armor of God. Every warrior of old put on his armor even though he had complete confidence in his general. Protective armor is always heavy, cumbersome, and difficult to put on, but warriors know that their lives depend on it. In today's world football players wear pads and helmets, police put on bullet-proof vests, and soldiers wear body armor for protection. Yet how many churches go into battle unprepared because they simply take for granted that all will turn out for the best, rather than intentionally clothing themselves with their means of defense?

Before looking at the individual parts of our armor, we need to look at the passage as a whole.

First, these words are addressed to the church as the body of Christ collectively, and not only to individuals. To be sure, they have an individual application, as is true of all exhortations concerning the church. Few churches, however, seem to understand that this passage is a statement of God's strategy for the church to prevail against the enemy. Churches, as well as individuals, can become enslaved in spiritual bondage. The odds are great, for Satan is unceasing in his efforts to take God's children captive to do *his* will (2 Timothy 2:26). When churches fail to identify their true adversary, the consequences are disastrous.

Second, these words are a revelation not only of how the church is to resist the forces of evil, but they also provide an insight into the nature of Satan's schemes. Each part of the armor identifies Satan's target of attack, as well as the church's means of defense. Satan and his angels will attack the church primarily with respect to truth, righteousness, the good news of peace, faith, and salvation.

Third, each element of our armor has both an objective and subjective application. Overcoming the schemes of the enemy entails both *trusting* the unshakable foundation of our salvation and actively *obeying* the Lord's commandments. To resist the devil we are to stand on God's truth, but we are also to speak the truth. We are to be covered by Christ's righteousness, but we are also to live righteously. We have the certainty of being at peace with God, but we are to take the gospel of peace to others. Faith is not only belief in our Lord; it is intimate relationship with Him. Salvation is more than becoming a child of God; it is affirming our legal position in Christ.

## The belt of truth

Paul uses the imagery of the armor of the Roman soldier to illustrate our spiritual armor. The first item is the belt, or girdle, which held the rest of the armor in place, including the sword. In the same way, everything in our spiritual warfare hangs on the commitment of the church to truth. When we say truth, we mean something that has objective reality; we are not referring to mere subjective opinion. We stand against the schemes of the devil by our commitment to unshakable truth.

The church is not founded on a philosophy of religion; the church is established on hard historic facts. As Luke said in the beginning of his gospel, these facts were reported by eye-witnesses; they could be investigated, and therefore verified. The birth of Jesus was not folklore; He was born miraculously of a young woman who was a virgin, in a specific place, at a specific time in the history of the world. He lived a real life; people saw Him, touched Him, listened to Him talk. His miracles were seen by thousands; the immediate cause of His arrest and subsequent condemnation was that His enemies could not disprove the raising of Lazarus from the dead. He died on a cross that was just as real as the thousands on which others suffered crucifixion. Had you run your hand over it, you would have gotten real splinters. He was buried in a real tomb. On the third day He came out of the tomb alive, physically raised from the dead. His disciples touched Him; He took food and ate. He was seen not only by His disciples and friends, but by more than 500 people at one time, most of whom were still alive when Paul wrote about it, meaning they could be questioned (1 Corinthians 15:3-6).

> *Many Christians are turning away from the very concept of truth itself*

When what was termed "the new Catholicism" began to be propagated in Europe, I attended a conference on the resurrection given by one of their theologians. In his remarks he said, with passion, that he believed in the resurrection so profoundly that had he gone into the tomb on Easter Sunday and found the dead body of the Lord, his faith in the resurrection would not have been shaken. At that statement there were heads shaken by many of his hearers who were not intellectual enough to comprehend how a body can be dead and alive at the same moment.

The gospel by which we are saved is not based on fables, but reality. Paul states plainly that if Jesus was not raised, we are without hope. Everything in our spiritual armor is held together by truth.

In a previous generation those who wished to deny the truths of the Christian faith attempted to do so rationally, attacking either the credibility of those who were eyewitnesses or the authenticity of their writings. In their effort to overturn the truths of our faith these skeptics did not abandon the reality of objective truth, however; they still lived in the real world. You could sit down with them and reason.

Perhaps the greatest tragedy of a growing segment of the church in our times, however, is the progressive abandoning of the very reality of objective truth. Succumbing to post-modern philosophies, large numbers of those who call themselves Christians are turning away not only from certain *truths,* but from the very concept of truth itself. For many, truth is not found in the intent of the writer of Scripture, but in the subjective interpretation of the reader.

This does nothing less than pave the way for the great delusion of the lawless one.

> The coming of the lawless one will be in accordance with the work of Satan displayed in all kinds of counterfeit miracles, signs, and wonders, and in every sort of evil that deceives those who are perishing. They perish *because they refused to love the truth* and so be saved. For this reason God sends them a powerful delusion so that they will believe the lie and so that all will be condemned who have not believed the truth but have delighted in wickedness (2 Thessalonians 2:9-12, emphasis added).

If we did not know the end of the story, we would be tempted to think that Satan and his angels are succeeding in their attack against truth in all her forms. Anyone who has the courage to affirm that our Lord Jesus Christ is *the* truth and *the* only way to know God soon finds himself in full-fledged conflict against the world, the flesh, and the devil. Here, however, there can be no compromise.

Whenever the church, or its members, unbuckles the belt of truth, the entire armor of God falls to the ground, and the principalities and powers of the unseen world are free to fulfill Satan's insidious schemes unopposed.

## The breastplate of righteousness

The term "devil" means *accuser.* Satan is the great accuser. The object of his accusations is the very foundation of God's throne: how could a God of righteousness dare express His love to those who have violated His holiness? Revelation 12:10 states that the accuser of our brothers accuses them before God day and night.

Yet though Satan continues his accusations, they have been emptied of their force. Jesus took all our sins upon Himself in dying on the cross, and we are now justified, declared righteous by God. Our Lord Himself is our advocate (1 John 2:1). Having no more basis to accuse us before God, however, Satan directs his accusations against us personally, seeking to overcome us with guilt and defeat.

When looking at their past, many believers struggle with regret. At times those regrets are focused on things that are fairly insignificant, but have the potential of becoming obsessive. Such obsessions are not only debilitating, but they represent chinks in the armor that allow the devil's forces to reach into the very heart of the believer and establish a foothold. In the face of these attacks it is useless to merely seek to put those regrets out of our mind or to try to justify our past mistakes. It is only as we see ourselves as clothed in the righteousness of our Lord Jesus Christ that we can stand firm against the schemes of the enemy.

We are justified through faith, not through our works. God has declared us righteous by clothing us with the righteousness of our Lord, stripping away the filthy rags of the past. Standing in the righteousness of Christ, we have the unspeakable privilege of standing firm against the devil's accusations.

Though the breastplate of righteousness refers primarily to our standing in Christ, we believers must never forget that Satan and his angels will also attack us with respect to our personal righteousness, tempting us to sin. In Paul's letters to the early churches he follows his truth passages with instructions concerning personal holiness. Sinful behavior opens the door to satanic influence and even control, resulting in bondage. There must be no cracks in the breastplate of the Christian. Any cracks must be closed immediately through repentance, confession, and forgiveness.

## The preparation of the gospel of peace

God's people must have their "feet fitted with the readiness that comes from the gospel of peace" (Ephesians 6:15). Believers must always be prepared to share the good news of peace. As Peter says, "But in your hearts set apart Christ as Lord. Always be prepared to give an answer to everyone who asks you to give the reason for the hope that you have" (1 Peter 3:15). We are to do so with gentleness and respect.

Hearing that warning, our first thought is that to withstand the attacks of the evil one, the church must always be in readiness to proclaim the message of salvation to the lost. Paul's words in Romans 10:15 seem to confirm that thought: "How beautiful are the feet of those who bring good news." It is obvious that as a body of "called out ones" (Greek *ekklesia*), the church must resist enemy attacks by continuing to call out a people for God's name. Proclaiming boldly the gospel of peace is one of our strongest defenses against Satan's attacks. In fact, Paul specifically asks for prayer that he might "fearlessly make known the mystery of the gospel" for which he was an ambassador in chains (Ephesians 6:19-20).

The application of this part of our armor, however, is doubtless not limited to evangelism. The gospel here is presented as the good news of *peace*. Being protected from hurtful accusations by the breastplate of righteousness, we walk with the assurance that we are at peace with God, both now and forever. "Therefore, there is now no condemnation for those who are in Christ Jesus" (Romans 8:1). Because of this,

> in all these things we are more than conquerors through Him who loved us. [We are] convinced that neither death nor life, neither angels nor demons, neither the present nor the future, nor any *powers*, neither height nor depth, nor anything in all creation, will be able to separate us from the love of God which is in Christ Jesus our Lord (Romans 8:37-39, emphasis added).

We are at peace with God; can there be any better news than this?

There is even a further application concerning having our feet shod with the gospel of peace. In reflecting on Paul's letter to the Ephesians, we are impressed by the many references to peace with respect to the church. He exhorts the church to make every effort to maintain the unity of the body through the bond of *peace* (Ephesians 4:3).

> The Lord himself is our *peace*, who has made the two one and has destroyed the barrier, the dividing wall of hostility, by abolishing in his flesh the law with its commandments and regulations. His purpose was to create in himself one new man out of the two, thus making *peace*, and in this one body to reconcile both of them to God through the

cross, by which he put to death their hostility. He came and preached *peace* to you who were far away and *peace* to those who were near. For through Him we both have access to the Father by one Spirit (Ephesians 2:14-18, emphasis added).

> The church characterized by conflict and disunity is an easy prey for Satan

The words of Jesus in the Sermon on the Mount, "Blessed are the peacemakers" (Matthew 5:9), have a prophetic ring. A church characterized by conflict and disunity is an easy prey for Satan. Satan's vicious attacks are not only against the church's commitment to truth and righteousness. He also strikes the church where she is most vulnerable—her commitment to peace. When members of the body of Christ forget that the conflict is not against flesh and blood, and begin to turn on each other, their ability to take the good news to the world is hopelessly compromised.

## The shield of faith

Satan and his angels are continually shooting the fiery darts of doubt at the church. The church must continually protect herself behind the shield of faith; some of those fiery darts cast doubt on the very basis of the faith. Throughout history churches have been toppled from their foundations by the seductive doctrines of demons, just as they will be in the end times (1 Timothy 4:1).

For churches whose commitment to truth is solid, however, Satan has adopted a different strategy—that of replacing faith in the Lord with self-sufficiency and with the desire to fight against Satan's fiery darts through our own resources. The apostle Paul was well aware of this danger. In 2 Corinthians 3:5 he acknowledges, "Not that we are competent in ourselves to claim anything for ourselves, but our competence comes from God."

In his first letter to the Corinthians he writes:

When I came to you ... I did not come with eloquence or superior wisdom as I proclaimed to you the testimony about God. For I resolved to know nothing while I was with you except Jesus Christ and him crucified. I came to you in weakness and fear, and with much trembling. My message and my preaching were not with wise and persuasive words, but with a demonstration of the Spirit's power, so that your faith might not rest on men's wisdom, but on God's power (1 Corinthians 2:1-5).

This passage is a good example of faith in action—faith that is more than intellectual belief but total confidence on the Lord. "I live by faith in the son of God," said Paul in his famous passage about being crucified with Christ (Galatians 2:20).

In his prayer for the church in Ephesus he prayed that Christ would dwell in their hearts by faith (Ephesians 3:17). This is far more than an expression of belief in the Lord for salvation; it is a way of life both for the church collectively and for believers individually.

Faith is total confidence in the Lord expressed *in a state of continual relationship*. It is complete trust in the one who Himself has promised to build His church. Only this kind of faith will protect us from the fiery darts of the evil one.

> *Faith is total confidence in the Lord expressed in a state of continual relationship*

The opposite of faith is independence. Just as independence was the essence of the first sin, independence continues to be the essence of all sin against God, including the sin of self-reliance. Probably at no time in history has the church been attacked by the temptation of self-reliance more than today, when churches have so easily been transformed into corporations. Too many of the churches' tools, provided through endless conferences and manuals, encourage believers

117

to put their confidence in the methods of this world rather than in the power of the Spirit.

The pathetic words of the prophet Jeremiah could well apply to much of the church today: "My people have committed two sins: They have forsaken me, the spring of living water, and have dug their own cisterns, broken cisterns that cannot hold water" (Jeremiah 2:13).

## The helmet of salvation

We have seen that in our spiritual warfare everything hangs on the commitment of the church to truth—objective reality, not mere subjective reasoning. We do not stand against the schemes of the devil through power encounters, but through truth encounters. The *belt of truth* seems to designate truth in general; the *helmet of salvation* points more specifically to the truths of our relationship to Christ in salvation.

It is obvious that Paul is using the term *salvation* in a broader sense than just being saved from our sin and given eternal life. In the New Testament salvation refers to the totality of our redemption—the truth that Satan was stripped of his authority at the cross; the truth that we have been raised up and are seated with Christ in the heavens, outranking Satan in spiritual authority; the truth that greater is He that is in us than he that is in the world; the truth that when we resist Satan and his angels, they have no recourse but to flee from us.

It is significant that the helmet of salvation protects the head, which is the seat of the mind, the principal target of Satan's attacks and where Satan's attacks are the most vicious. Satan establishes his strongholds in the mind. The helmet of salvation protects us not only from any doubts about our eternal salvation; it also protects us from the continual blows of Satan in our day-by-day struggles.

In a parallel passage Paul calls the helmet the *hope* of salvation (1 Thessalonians 5:8). This reference reveals yet another aspect of Satan's schemes. As we have seen, the enemy has neutralized untold numbers of believers through self-confidence and pride. When this tactic fails, however, his attacks turn to the other extreme, stripping away all shreds of confidence and bringing them to a sense of utter worthlessness. Hopelessness leads to despair. No soldier can go into battle without hope of victory. The believer must remember that in himself he can do nothing, but that must not cause him to forget that he can choose to do all things through Christ who strengthens him (Philippians 4:13).

Hope is the amazing complement to faith. Faith delivers us from *pride*, enabling us to place our total confidence in the Lord and His ability to do immeasurably more than all we could ever ask or even imagine. Hope delivers us from *despair* by reminding us that God will do this "according to his power that is at work *within us*" (Ephesians 3:20, emphasis added).

Truth, righteousness, gospel, faith, salvation—they are the elements of the armor that protect us from the devil's schemes. In this struggle, however, we are not only to stand, we must advance, not in our own ingenuity, but with the weapons provided by our King. In the next chapter we will consider our chief instrument of attack— the sword of the Spirit. *The Word of God*

## Discussion questions:

Why is the church the prime target of Satan?

How does Paul's account of the spiritual armor help us better understand the strategy of Satan?

Explain why faith is not just intellectual belief.

# Chapter Thirteen

# Brandishing Truth

*The sword of the Spirit, which is the Word of God, is the piece of armor that enables the church to go on the offensive against the powers of darkness. Our example is the Lord Himself, who countered every temptation with the authority of God's Word. The Word of God becomes our weapon against the strongholds of Satan, who continues to use the world, the flesh, and the powers of darkness to oppose the believer.*

NO ONE SHOULD BE SURPRISED BY THE CONTINUAL ATTACKS on the church by her archenemy. Like a roaring lion, the devil prowls around, constantly seeking to devour (1 Peter 5:8). What is surprising is that churches continually forget that their battle is not against flesh and blood. Satan and his angels manipulate believers into allowing even insignificant squabbles to become major conflicts.

The invisibility of the enemy makes Satan's attacks all the more insidious. He delights when churches spend their resources fighting the wrong battles. Blessed are the churches that have been trained to immediately arm themselves with God's armor to stand against the deception of the devil. Strength comes only from the Lord and the power of His might.

In the previous chapter we examined the first five components of this armor: the belt of truth, the breastplate of righteousness, feet shod with the preparation of the gospel of peace, the shield of faith,

> *The sword of the Spirit is our principal weapon of attack against the devil*

and the helmet of salvation. They have one thing in common—they are mainly defensive. They keep us from collapsing under the onslaughts of the evil one.

In this chapter our attention will turn to something that is both defensive and offensive—the sword of the Spirit, the Word of God. The church must do more than stand; she must resist. The devil cannot prevail when we resist him on the authority of Christ with God's divinely appointed weapon, the sword of the Spirit.

In the New Testament two different words are translated "sword." A *machira* is a short sword, or a dagger. A *rhomphira* is larger, and can refer to a spear. The use of the former word in this passage emphasizes close proximity to the enemy. It is underscored by the fact that we are *wrestling* against the principalities and powers of darkness, indicating close-quarter combat (Ephesians 6:12, NKJV). In fact, our combat with Satan takes place in the mind; it is in the mind that our enemy establishes his strongholds.

The sword of the Spirit, the Word of God, is our principal weapon of attack against the devil. For those who know the Scriptures, Paul's reference to the Word of God as the sword of the Spirit immediately recalls a parallel passage in Hebrews 4:12: "For the word of God is living and active. Sharper than any double-edged sword, it penetrates even to dividing soul and spirit, joints and marrow; it judges the thoughts and attitudes of the heart." In both passages the Word of God is compared to a sword that has the capacity to pierce.

In the Greek text, however, there is a notable difference. Though both passages speak of the *Word* of God, the terms translated *word* are not the same. The Hebrews passage uses the term *logos,* whereas the Ephesians passage uses the term *rema. Logos* puts emphasis on the Word in its *essence,* whereas *rema* stresses the Word in its *expression* or usage. When Paul tells us to take the sword of the Spirit, which is the Word of God, he is telling us to actively use it. That implies that the believer must not only *know* the Word, but he must also be able to *apply* it and allow it to penetrate the strongholds that the enemy has established in the mind.

Our prime model for using God's Word as the sword of the Spirit is, of course, our Lord in His combat with Satan during His temptation. The more we reflect on this amazing account the more it astounds us. It was a conflict totally unlike anything the world had ever seen or would ever see in the future. Here was Satan, once the most exalted of the angelic beings, who had become the most despicable through his rebellion against God. He was the legal prince of this world, having usurped the authority originally given to Adam. Facing him was his Creator, the eternal Word of God, now incarnated as a man, facing him in the same vulnerable human form that the devil despised when he was made the protector of Adam.

As the eternal Son of God, our Lord, with one word from His mouth, could have totally banished Satan from the earth and consigned him to the lake of fire. Yet to do so would have terminated any hope for the redemption of the human race and shaken the very throne of the God of love and justice. Jesus had to win this battle as a man, subject to His heavenly Father.

How did Jesus triumph over Satan? Through the written Word of God. Even though He Himself was the *eternal* Word, as a man He took the sword of the Spirit and plunged it into Satan's crafty schemes. "It is written," began our Lord after each temptation. Satan even made a feeble attempt to trick our Lord by citing Scripture himself, but that was only a parody (Matthew 4:6).

The first battle had been lost when Adam and Eve refused to submit to God's stated word and affirmed their independence. The battle between Satan and Jesus was won simply and decisively by Jesus' use of the sword of the Spirit.

## Satan's strongholds

As already mentioned, the enemy's main strongholds are established in the mind. To be sure, Satan's field of battle is vast, requiring constant vigilance every day of our lives in every area of society—family, church, business, or government. He is relentless in his attacks. Yet the front lines of the battle are always in the thoughts and intents of the heart of man. We must constantly "demolish arguments and every pretension that sets itself up against the knowledge of God." We must "take captive every thought and make it obedient to Christ" (2 Corinthians 10:5). This refers both to the thoughts that invade our own minds and to the philosophies that invade the church as a whole. "Though we live in the world, we do not wage war as the world does. The weapons we fight with are not the weapons of the world. On the contrary, they have divine power to demolish strongholds" (2 Corinthians 10:3-4).

> *The enemy's main strongholds are those that are established in the mind*

Just what are the strongholds of the evil one, specifically, and what is the role of the sword of the Spirit in tearing them down?

We saw in chapter 9 that Satan's schemes grow out of the three principal enemies of the church: the world, the flesh, and demonic powers. In this chapter we will see how Satan uses the three enemies to establish strongholds in the mind, and how to effectively combat them with the sword of the Spirit. We will learn how to use the Word of God specifically and to take captive every thought and make it obedient to Christ.

It is tragic that, though believers in our evangelical churches have an abundance of knowledge *about* Scripture, too much of that knowledge remains cognitive and compartmentalized. Studies of believers' worldview reveal that only a minority of Christians are able to personalize their knowledge into a worldview that enables them to recognize the strongholds of Satan and effectively combat them.

### Strongholds related to the world

Satan, as the god of this world (2 Corinthians 4:4), has blinded the minds of unbelievers so that they cannot see the light of the gospel. As god of this world, however, he is also skilled at blinding the minds of believers, and of the church as a whole, distorting their value system and enslaving them in a world system that is in opposition to the purpose of God.

Satan uses three strongholds in the world's system: *power, possessions*, and *pleasure* to take captive the thoughts of mankind. Though the wise Solomon eloquently showed that those three strongholds are vanity and that to seek after them is no more than the pursuit of the wind (Ecclesiastes 1 and 2), they remain the preoccupation of the majority of the world's population and the basis of the world's culture.

It is fascinating that in one short discourse our Lord provides powerful swords to combat each of those strongholds. We are referring of course to what we call the Sermon on the Mount, recorded in Matthew 5-7. The theme of our Lord's powerful words is in Matthew 6:33: "But seek first his kingdom and his righteousness, and all these things will be given to you as well."

> *Brandishing the sword of the Spirit means having a biblical worldview*

In that sermon Jesus touches on every aspect of the world's values. To those seeking power, He says, "Blessed are the meek." To those seeking possessions, He says, "Do not store up for yourselves treasures on earth." To those seeking pleasure as an end in itself, He says, "Wide is the gate, and broad is the road that leads to destruction."

Brandishing the sword of the Spirit means having a biblical worldview—seeing the world through the Word of God, making the Word of God personal, and plunging it into the strongholds of the evil one. To do so is not politically correct; it has the potential of inviting misunderstanding and even opposition from friends, family, and fellow believers. But the stakes are too high to allow compromise. When faced with such opposition, we remember the words of our Lord: "Blessed are those who are persecuted because of righteousness, for theirs is the kingdom of heaven" (Matthew 5:10).

## Strongholds related to the flesh

As we saw in chapter 9, the term "flesh" in the New Testament often does not refer to the physical part of man, but to the sinful nature— moral sickness that comes from separation from God and the resulting disintegration of our very beings. Just as the devil as the god of this world has succeeded in conforming the world into submission to his reprehensible desires, he also uses the world and its values to manipulate the desires of sinful man.

1 John 2:15-17 states it clearly:

> Do not love the world or anything in the world. If anyone loves the world, the love of the Father is not in him. For everything in the world—the cravings of sinful man, the lust of his eyes and the boasting of what he has and does—comes not from the Father but from the world. The world and its desires pass away, but the man who does the will of God lives forever.

It is remarkable to see the close correlation in this passage between the values of the world and the temptations of the flesh. The world esteems *power*, which in turn incites man's lust of the eyes. The world treasures *possessions*, which in turn incites man's boasting of what he has and does. The world seeks *pleasure*, which increasingly incites the cravings of sinful man.

When we move from the *world* to the *flesh*, however, we see that Satan's strongholds easily move from the purely cognitive area of man's mind to his obsessions. It is one thing to rationally discuss the world with its values and to come to certain conclusions. It is far different when the world's values are transformed into compulsive behavior and obsessive thought patterns.

When Satan's evil hierarchy succeeds in breaking through our protective armor, creating strongholds in our minds, we will not succeed in tearing down these strongholds with the weapons of this world. Purely secular psychology, coupled with all the counseling available, will never get to the root of the problem. We must turn to the sword of the Spirit, which is the Word of God. Only truth empowered by God's Spirit will deliver us from the obsessive behavior provoked by evil beings.

> *To use the sword of the Spirit effectively is to walk in the Spirit*

Many Christians who had become enslaved by lustful thoughts, for example, bear testimony that their only path to freedom was to memorize Scripture passages concerning purity and to combat every sinful thought with the sword of the Spirit, all the time reaffirming their having been seated with Christ in the heavenlies.

Brandishing the sword of the Spirit, however, is far more than merely quoting Bible verses, though too many believers are not even capable of doing that. The Word of God is the sword *of the Spirit*. Bible verses are not magic wands to be waved over our temptations. *For God's Spirit to manifest His power, our spirits must be united with the truth of the Word through authentic submission and obedience.* Theoretical knowledge about the Word will not cut it. The Spirit's power is released only when there is conscious surrender to the God of the Word.

To use the sword of the Spirit effectively is to walk in the Spirit in order to not gratify the desires of the sinful nature. That means willful obedience, not just warm feelings. "The fruit of the Spirit is love, joy, peace, patience, kindness, goodness, faithfulness, gentleness, and self-control" (Galatians 5:22-23). In reading this impressive list, however, we should not get the idea that the fruit of the Spirit is like fruit effortlessly growing on a tree. Every quality of the fruit of the Spirit is related to commands in God's Word that are to be prayerfully obeyed. There must be more than mere knowledge; there must be commitment. When my spirit, and not just my brain, unites with God's Word in active obedience, God's Spirit is unleashed in me, bringing freedom.

## Strongholds related to satanic powers

We now come to the most malicious of the strongholds of evil—strongholds created by the very invasion of demonic powers into the minds of men and women. Scripture makes it plain that every true believer is the temple of the Holy Spirit. On the other hand, not every believer is filled with the Holy Spirit; otherwise the commandment in Ephesians to be filled, or controlled, by the Spirit would have no meaning (Ephesians 5:18). Believers can be trapped by the devil, and can be taken captive to do his will (2 Timothy 2:26).

Though it is true that the New Testament does not use the term "possessed" when referring to demonic influence on people (they are said to be "demonized"), examples of demonic activity in the lives of professing believers are widespread. Thousands of Christians are in need of deliverance from spiritual bondage.

The last four decades have seen a proliferation of every kind of occult activity, associated with widespread use of drugs and unnatural sexual activity. Christians who work among students face this challenge almost daily. A young African Christian who had come to America to enroll in a secular university came to me some time ago, seeking to transfer to a school which conformed to his convictions. "I left Africa to *get away* from witchcraft," he said. "I do not want to get back into it in my college dormitory."

Just as Jesus used the sword of the Spirit to effectively overcome Satan, so must every believer. Providentially God has raised up servants whose eyes are open to the realities of the unseen world and its devastating consequences on many believers. Though some have gone to extremes in their fascination with "power encounters" and "casting out demons," others have helped many thousands of believers to know how to use the sword of the Spirit in a way that brings freedom in Christ through the affirmation of our position in Christ.

The sword of the Spirit is available to all believers, great and small. It must not be left in its sheath. It is to be used.

The ministry of Dr. Neil Anderson, founder of Freedom in Christ ministries (*ficm.org*), has been instrumental in helping thousands of Christians worldwide to break the chains of spiritual bondage and find their rightful freedom in Christ. Dr. Anderson puts emphasis on truth encounters, rather than power encounters. His definitive work, *The Bondage Breaker* (Harvest House), contains an effective tool that enables believers to brandish the sword of the Spirit through repentance, confession, renunciation, and resistance. This tool, called *The Steps to Freedom in Christ*, brings deliverance by enabling believers to affirm their position in Christ.

## Discussion questions:

What does Satan's temptation of Jesus teach us about using the sword of the Spirit?

How must we use the sword of the Spirit to prevent Satan from establishing strongholds in our minds?

What are practical ways of transforming our knowledge of the Word of God into a spiritual weapon against the schemes of Satan?

# Chapter Fourteen

# Praying Always

*Underlying and empowering all the elements of the church's spiritual armor is prayer. Believers are to pray always with all kinds of prayers and petitions for all the saints. Through prayer they occupy their spiritual inheritance on which the forces of darkness are illegally squatting. Prayer is the church's means of seeking legal rights from the great Judge and opening doors into the church's spiritual inheritance.*

THE CHURCH IS ENGAGED IN CONFLICT WITH AN INVISIBLE enemy that seeks her destruction—that is *why* we must be strong in the Lord and in the power of His might. To be strong in the Lord, we must put on the whole armor or God—that is *what* we must do in order to stand firm against this invisible enemy. We are to "pray in the Spirit on all occasions with all kinds of prayers and requests"— that is *how* we put on God's armor (Ephesians 6:18).

Nowhere else in the Bible do we find a statement concerning prayer that is more all-inclusive than that. "And Paul goes on to say, "With this in mind, be alert and always keep on praying for all the Lord's people." We are to pray on *all* occasions, with *all kinds* of prayers and requests, at *all* times, for *all* the saints. Prayer is not only indispensable as the means of clothing ourselves with the armor of God, it is also the principal means of engaging in conflict with the principalities and powers of evil. Our example is Paul's coworker Epaphras, who was "always *wrestling* in prayer" (Colossians 4:12, emphasis added).

Nothing is more clear in the Scriptures than that we are to persevere in prayer. Prayer must permeate our existence. Meditate for a few moments on the following passages:

Romans 12:12: we are to be "faithful in prayer."

Colossians 4:2: we are to "devote [ourselves] to prayer."

Philippians 4:6: we are "to present [our] requests to God in everything, by prayer and petition, with thanksgiving."

1 Thessalonians 5:17: we are to "pray continually."

1 Timothy 2:1: Paul urges that "requests, prayers, intercession, and thanksgiving be made for everyone." And Paul himself was a demonstration of this perseverance, for again and again he reveals how, at each remembrance of the churches, he brought them to the throne in thanksgiving and prayer (e.g. Philippians 1:6).

> *Prayer is the means of moving from the visible to the invisible dimension of our spiritual conflict*

These appeals to continual prayer raise questions for some believers, however. *Why* must we persevere in prayer? We know God hears us the first time we ask Him for something. We know that He does not need to be constantly reminded of what we ask. We know that He does not have to be convinced by our persistence.

The answer is that the conflict with the forces of darkness is real. Prayer is the means of moving from the visible into the hidden dimension of our spiritual conflict. It is the means of penetrating beyond the veil and infusing spiritual energy into that mysterious domain of the spirits where the real battles are being fought. We can only imagine what forces are unleashed on the world of darkness when we pray.

Revelation 8 gives us a glimpse of this kind of power. The chapter tells of an angel with a golden censer standing at the golden altar before God's throne. He was given incense along with the prayers of all the saints to offer on the altar. When the smoke of the incense and the saints' prayers went up before God, the angel took the censer, filled it with fire from the altar, and hurled it to the earth, bringing peals of thunder, rumblings, flashes of lightning, and an earthquake (Revelation 8:3-5). The symbolism of this vision is striking. Though our prayers rise to the Lord with the gentleness of incense, God's answers have the power of thunder, rumblings, flashes of lightning, and earthquakes.

This passage offers some valuable insights concerning Scripture's repeated exhortations to permeate our ministries with prayer. When we pray, our requests go directly to the throne of God without any impediment. Through prayer every believer, no matter who he is, can lift his soul to God and be in direct communication with the Creator and sustainer of the universe.

The situation is entirely different with respect to God's answers to our prayers. His answers face a veritable obstacle course. There is supernatural opposition from the invisible forces of evil.

The classic example of this opposition is God's answer to the prayer of Daniel in chapter 10 of his prophecy. After mourning for three weeks, Daniel was met by the heavenly messenger sent from God. The words of this messenger are astonishing:

Do not be afraid, Daniel. Since the first day that you set your mind to gain understanding and to humble yourself before your God, your words were heard, and I have come in response to them. But the prince of the Persian kingdom resisted me twenty-one days. Then Michael, one of the chief princes, came to help me, because I was detained there with the king of Persia (Daniel 10:12-13).

Many would think it incredible that a messenger sent from God could face that kind of resistance. Yet the passage shows us that the world is not a huge marionette stage with God calmly pulling all the strings. The world is a battlefield with the church in continual struggle against the principalities and powers of evil in her mission of calling out and perfecting a people for the name of the Lord. The conflict is real; this is not science fiction. Some battles are won, and some are lost. Persevering prayer determines the difference.

## The story of the widow

The parable of the widow in Luke 18 addresses the need for praying without ceasing. The purpose of the parable is clearly stated in the first verse: "Jesus told His disciples a parable to show them that they should always pray and not give up." Then He proceeded to tell them about a widow who kept coming to a judge to seek her legal rights against her adversary. The judge was an egotistical man "who neither feared God nor cared about men" (v. 2). He kept refusing to listen to her, but finally said to himself, "Even though I don't fear God or care about men, yet because this widow keeps bothering me, I will see that she gets justice, so that she won't eventually wear me out with her coming!"

This parable is confusing to many who read it. Is God like the unjust judge who must be pestered by His children before He will grant their request? Not at all. He delights in answering the prayers of His children.

To understand a parable we must focus on the main point and simply allow the rest of the story to fill in the details. The purpose of the parable is to emphasize the need of persistence in prayer. The main point of the parable is not the *reticence* of the unjust judge, but the *request* of the persistent widow. She was seeking her legal rights.

We are not told the circumstances of the widow's plight. We can only imagine that upon the death of her husband, she received an inheritance she could not claim, perhaps because of squatters—a common occurrence in many countries. Unable in her own strength to claim her rights, she had to appeal to her legal rights until her request was granted.

The plight of the widow is strikingly similar to the plight of every believer. We have been given an inheritance. Our mission is to occupy our inheritance. The inheritance, however, is occupied by squatters who have unbelievable power. Yet these squatters have no legal right to any part of our inheritance. For us to occupy what is legally ours, we must constantly come before the great Judge to claim it.

### We have an inheritance in God's plan

Ephesians 1:11 states that we have an inheritance in God's plan; a literal translation is "*in Him we were assigned a lot.*" The NASB gives this translation: "in Him also we have obtained an inheritance." The context plainly relates this "lot" to God's administration of the fullness of times, revealing that we have been assigned a share in God's great plan of bringing together all things, both visible and invisible, under the headship of Christ (Ephesians 1:9-10). Though most references concerning our inheritance refer to the future, Ephesians 1:11 clearly refers to something we have already been given. Our present inheritance is not land or possessions; it is people.

> *To occupy what is legally ours, we must constantly come before the great Judge to claim it*

It is unfortunate that some of our translations identify the expression "fullness of the times" in Ephesians 1:10 (NASB) exclusively with the millennial kingdom. This is to forget that the "fullness of times" began when God poured out His Spirit at Pentecost. Any doubt about that should be wiped away when we come to the end of the chapter, where we are told that this fullness manifests itself in the church, which is the body of Christ, "the fullness of him who fills [present tense] everything in every way" (Ephesians 1:23).

God's plan for this present age is to gather together all things under the headship of our Lord Jesus Christ, who is given to the church as head of all things. This plan of God is taking place both in the heavens and on the earth; those terms designate both the visible, seen world, and the invisible spirit world. It is God's purpose that through the church, armed with divinely-provided armor and wrestling in prayer, the authority of the Lord will be established by progressively bringing all things under His headship.

> *Spiritual warfare is not a once-and-for-all event; it is continual conflict*

The implications of this passage are enormous. Just as the children of Israel were given an inheritance in the Promised Land, we have a present inheritance in God's great plan among the nations. Our mission as believers does not consist in seeking to carve out our own ministry. It is to occupy our assigned lot in God's great plan. This inheritance is related to our lives, our families, our churches, and our ministries.

### Our inheritance is occupied by enemy forces

When the children of Israel crossed the Jordan to occupy their legal inheritance, they immediately encountered the enemy. Struggle ensued and continued for many years. We can imagine that when the widow in Jesus' parable went to occupy her inheritance, it was occupied by the squatters. She was powerless to obtain what was legally hers without the intervention of a higher authority.

Throughout this book we have seen again and again how Satan, having become the legal prince of this world, extended his influence from the Garden of Eden throughout the entire world, continually leading to the corruption of entire peoples and provoking the retaliation of a just and holy God. Yet until the cross of our Lord, Satan operated legally, even though this legality was obtained by trickery.

Satan, though now dethroned, has not yet been banished from squatting on our inheritance. Our enemy continues to exercise his power as the god of this age. He establishes strongholds in believers' minds through such things as pride, envy, and a refusal to forgive. The latter is certainly one of his most effective tactics.

Whether as a roaring lion or an angel of light, Satan is determined to occupy our inheritance. If you have any doubts about his pervasive influence, go back to chapter 10 and review the New Testament references to his dark activity.

## *The enemy has been stripped of all legality*

Just before our Lord's Last Supper in the upper room, Jesus uttered this momentous statement, "Now is the time for judgment on this world; now the prince of this world will be driven out" (John 12:31). A little later, in the upper room, Jesus spoke of the coming of the Spirit, who would convict the world regarding sin, righteousness, and judgment—judgment *"because the prince of this world now stands condemned"* (John 16:11, emphasis added).

In this passage it is apparent that Jesus was referring to the legal condemnation of Satan, referred to in Colossians 2:15, where our Lord disarmed the powers and authorities, making a public spectacle of them, triumphing over them by the cross. The passage does not refer to his future imprisonment in the abyss, or his final judgment in the lake of fire.

We must remember that the disarming of Satan at the cross did not take away his power. Paul's description of our spiritual warfare in Ephesians 6 makes that abundantly clear. Satan still exercises formidable power as the archenemy of God, but he does so illegally. As we have seen, he has been stripped of his princely insignia, and his sword has been broken. He has been led as a prisoner in our Lord's triumphal procession and humiliated before the watching cosmos.

Is Satan squatting on our inheritance? Is he wreaking havoc in our minds, our families, our churches, our ministry? Though he might be unleashing all the powers available to him, he is the great deceiver. He has no legal rights to our part in God's great plan of bringing together all things under the headship of Christ. We outrank Satan and all his angels.

## *Prayer allows us to occupy our inheritance*

That brings us to the main point of the parable of the widow, which is that she had to come to the judge *continually* to obtain her legal rights.

In the case of the widow, it was because the judge did not want to be bothered, which is in no way the case with our heavenly Judge, the loving Lord who takes delight in the requests of His children. In our case, we must continually seek God's justice because our adversary, though he has no legal rights, continues to seek to squat on our inheritance, using every tactic at his disposal to oppose us.

Spiritual warfare is not a once-and-for-all event; it is continual conflict. The demonic and angelic activity around us is rampant. We need not be fearful, for we are in Christ. Yet Ephesians 6:18 makes it abundantly clear that we must pray and pray continually in seeking to overcome the god of this world, whatever form he assumes.

In Psalm 2:7-8 the Lord Jehovah makes this prophetic utterance to His Son: "You are my Son; today I have become your Father. *Ask of me*, and I will make the nations your inheritance, the ends of the earth your possession" (emphasis added). As adopted sons of God we are "heirs of God and co-heirs with Christ" (Romans 8:17). As co-heirs with Jesus Christ we can enter fully into this promise, asking with confidence that God will allow us to occupy our rightful inheritance in Jesus Christ.

Prayer opens doors into our spiritual inheritance. Colossians 4:2-4 states, "Devote yourselves to prayer, being watchful and thankful. And pray for us, too, that God may open a door for our message, so that we may proclaim the mystery of Christ, for which I am in chains." When we who are God's children open the door of *our* hearts and churches to the Lord, who stands and knocks (Revelation 3:20), *He* opens doors that no man can close (Revelation 3:7).

"LORD, you have assigned me my portion and my cup; you have made my lot secure. The boundary lines have fallen for me in pleasant places; surely I have a delightful inheritance" (Psalm 16:5-6).

## Discussion questions:

Why must we pray continually?

What does the Scripture mean when it says we were assigned a "lot"?

How does prayer allow us to occupy our spiritual inheritance?

## Chapter Fifteen

# Delivering *the* Captives

*Though legally seated with Christ in the heavenlies, the members of Christ's kingdom are on this earth as ambassadors with the mission of calling the people of this world to submission to the King through faith in His sacrifice. Their mission is twofold: to confront people with the message of God, and to confront the forces of evil through prayer.*

GOD'S SECRET WEAPON, THE CHURCH, WAS UNVEILED ON the day of Pentecost. From that day until now, the church has been the focus of Satan's fiercest attacks, even though he knows that his doom is sealed. But just as our Lord led the captives of Hades in triumphal procession into paradise, He continues to lead the church into the world in triumphal procession over Satan and his angels (2 Corinthians 2:14). This triumphal procession penetrates the darkest domains of the god of this world.

The church, legally seated with Christ in heavenly places, is commissioned to go into the whole world, covered with authority and filled with power. Her mission is to deliver the captives (Acts 26:17-18, Colossians 1:13-14). It is not by the church's might or power that Satan continually meets his defeat. It is by the Spirit of the Lord as promised in Zechariah 4:6: "'Not by might nor by power, but by my Spirit,' says the LORD Almighty." The humiliation suffered by Satan did not end at the cross. It is repeated continually as the Lord demonstrates His wisdom to the powers of darkness through His triumphant church.

The church is in the world on mission. It is no mystery that throughout the centuries Satan's chief strategy has been to divert the church from her purpose. One of the first and most effective of his many tactics was to change the focus of the church from heaven to earth. When the Roman emperor Constantine made Christianity a state religion in 313, the church turned from her heavenly mission in order to seek to establish an earthly kingdom. When the emperor Theodosius proclaimed Christianity as the only legal religion in 380, all the inhabitants of the empire were forced to accept Christianity as their religion. As a result, the pagan objects of worship were transformed into Christian shrines and idols, bringing paganism into the institutional church. That provided a wide-open door to Satan and his angels through the occult practices that had thoroughly permeated the people.

Today the church faces many other snares, including the continual temptation of replacing the gospel of redemption with the gospel of social justice. To be sure, the Bible is very clear that the church is to reach out to the needy and to alleviate human suffering. Our mission, however, is not to usher in an earthly kingdom, but to deliver the captives of this earthly kingdom into the eternal kingdom of God's Son. Kingdom ministries must follow the orders of the King.

If the true church were primarily an institution, Satan would be able to focus his forces against her more effectively. The sad history of the institutional church is evidence of the success of that focus. But the church is not an institution; she is the body and bride of Christ, composed of millions of redeemed souls, each one a temple of the Spirit of God. When our enemy attacks on one front, the church spills out on another as the Spirit manifests His power, continually disorienting the devil and his cohorts.

## The church on mission

We saw in Ephesians 6 that the church is exhorted to *stand*—to stand firm against the continuous attacks of the enemy, fully clothed with the armor of God. The prevailing church, however, must do more than stand; she must press forward. The church is to penetrate the most foreboding domains of darkness, empowered by prayer and brandishing the sword of the Spirit. Even the gates of Hades, manned by the principalities and powers of the evil one, will not be able to prevail against her.

Last words always have immense importance, but never have last words been more significant than those of Jesus just before He was caught up to heaven from the Mount of Olives. We call those words the Great Commission, and they are the marching orders of the church. In one form or another, the Commission is repeated five times, once in each Gospel and once in the book of Acts.

> *The church is in the world on mission*

Our Lord's disciples had just asked Him whether that was the time He would establish His kingdom. In His answer Jesus emphasized that the time of the kingdom was not to be their preoccupation. It was not for them to know the times and dates that God had set by His authority. With all their hearts, they were to plunge into their new mission as ambassadors to the entire world, beginning at Jerusalem and extending to the ends of the earth.

The Spirit of the church is the Spirit of *mission*. To quench the Spirit of mission is to quench the Spirit of the church, for it is obvious that there is but one Holy Spirit. As the spiritual incarnation of our Lord, the church is missionary in her very essence. As stated earlier, by His first body our Lord *procured* salvation; by His spiritual body He *proclaims* salvation.

That means that the Great Commission is far more than an external command; it is a statement of the very life principle of the church. It is the church's fundamental law of existence. When I was a boy my mother often said, "Get your elbows off the table." That was an external command; I could prove that I was perfectly capable of eating with my elbows on the table. But when she said, "Eat your dinner," she was pronouncing a life principle. To refuse to eat would eventually bring death. The church is *ecclesia*, a body of called-out ones, and she can continue to exist only as she continues to pursue her life principle, the calling out a people for God's name.

Every church is destined to die either by stagnation or by germination. Churches that turn inward on themselves, isolating themselves from the world into which they have been sent, are destined to die by stagnation. Death by stagnation leads to disintegration, and thousands of churches have followed that path. On the other hand, churches that die by germination are churches that are willing to allow God to plant them in the world with all its muck and mire, losing their identity as seeds and germinating into plants that will push their roots down into our sinful societies and multiply. Death by germination does not mean extinction. It means that when a church is committed to her mission, she will constantly break out of her cultural shell, bringing new life.

> *Every church is destined to die either by stagnation or by germination*

Let us never think that the words of the Great Commission were meant only for the 500 or so disciples gathered around the Lord in Galilee—or let us never think that today they are meant only for a particular group of Christians we call missionaries. They are addressed to the church as a body, through the apostles, the church's appointed representatives. Because we are members of the body of Christ, those orders are for us personally. If we believe they are a statement of the church's fundamental purpose, we must also believe they are, by extension, a statement of the fundamental purpose of every believer.

### Authority and power

When we focus our attention on the statements of the Great Commission in Matthew and Acts, two terms capture our attention: authority and power. In Matthew 28:18-20 (emphasis added) Jesus gave this order to His worshiping followers:

> All *authority* in heaven and on earth has been given to me. Therefore go and make disciples of all nations, baptizing them in the name of the Father and of the Son and of the Holy Spirit, and teaching them to obey everything I have commanded you. And surely I am with you always, to the very end of the age.

Some would say that Jesus' use of the term "authority" merely means that He had the *right* to command His followers to go into the world and make disciples. That is true, of course —Jesus as our Lord has the right to give us whatever command He wishes.

When we examine the command in light of our struggle against principalities and powers, however, the term "authority" bursts with greater meaning. To go into the world is to penetrate the dominion of darkness so that men and women can be rescued "from the dominion of darkness and brought into the kingdom of the Son," as we have seen in Colossians 1:13. We can do this only as we are covered with the very authority of Jesus Christ—authority both in heaven, the domain of spirits, and on earth, the visible world of humans.

We who are the Lord's emissaries advance with the assurance that as ambassadors of Christ we are in Him, outranking Satan and his angels even in our weakest moments. We can say with the Psalmist, "O God the Lord, the strength of my salvation, You have covered my head in the day of battle" (Psalm 140:7, NKJV).

However, not only must our heads be covered in the day of battle by the *authority* of the Lord, we must be filled from within with *power* from His Spirit. Acts 1:8 says, "You will receive *power* when the Holy Spirit comes on you; and you will be my witnesses in Jerusalem, and in all Judea and Samaria, and to the ends of the earth" (emphasis added).

The interaction between power and witness is fascinating. On the one hand, we cannot effectively fulfill our mission as witnesses without being filled with the Spirit's power. On the other hand, nothing fills us with power more effectively than when we are authentic witnesses. Everyone who is faithful in making our Lord known can bear witness to the fact that when we are willing to make the Lord known, we sense His presence. In the film *Chariots of Fire*, Olympic sprinter Eric Liddell makes the famous statement, "God made me fast, and when I run, I feel his pleasure." God has made us His witnesses, and when we make Christ known, we feel His presence.

> Mission is more than confronting the lost with the message of salvation

One of Satan's most effective tactics is to distract us from the power of the Spirit and cause us to be preoccupied with our own wisdom and skill in seeking to fulfill our mission. The great missionary Paul makes it very clear that human wisdom is incapable of bringing men to salvation.

When I came to you . . . I did not come with eloquence or superior wisdom as I proclaimed to you the testimony about God. For I resolved to know nothing while I was with you except Jesus Christ and him crucified. I came to you in weakness and fear, and with much trembling. My message and my preaching were not with wise and persuasive words, *but with a demonstration of the Spirit's power*, so that your faith might not rest on men's wisdom, but on God's power (1 Corinthians 2:1-5, emphasis added).

## The two faces of mission

The missionary mandate of the church has two faces. Unfortunately, it seems that the majority of churches and even many missionaries are focused on only one. It is obvious that to make disciples means to confront the lost with the gospel of salvation. We have no problem understanding that, for we know that it is the gospel that is the power of salvation for all who believe, and as His witnesses we know that we are not to be ashamed of the gospel (Romans 1:16).

Mission, however, is more than confronting the lost with the message of salvation; it is also confronting the powers of darkness with God's authority and power through His Spirit. Paul clearly teaches that making disciples is not only opening people's eyes and turning them from darkness to light, but it is also rescuing them from the power of Satan (Acts 26:18).

Confronting the lost with the message of God's grace is only half the task; we are to engage in spiritual combat. This involves struggling in prayer to push back the forces of darkness and occupying our spiritual inheritance in the nations of the world.

Does that mean that we must be constantly preoccupied with the existence of evil spirits in everything we do? Of course not! It does mean, however, that we must constantly remember that "the whole world is in under the control of the evil one" (1 John 5:19), and that it is the god of this age who has blinded the minds of unbelievers "so that they cannot see the

> *The church is to invade the world of darkness and bondage with the message of freedom in Christ*

light of the gospel of the glory of Christ, who is the image of God" (2 Corinthians 4:4). Redemption is possible only through the authority of the risen Christ and the power of the Holy Spirit.

At the end of his account of our spiritual armor in Ephesians 6, Paul makes his urgent appeal for personal prayer. "Pray also for me," he says, "that whenever I open my mouth, words may be given me so that I will fearlessly make known the mystery of the gospel, for which I am an ambassador in chains. Pray that I may declare it fearlessly, as I should" (Ephesians 6:19-20). If Paul needed courage, how much more do we?

The mission of the church is clear: She is to invade the world of darkness and bondage with the message of freedom in Christ. As members of the body of Christ, we have an inheritance among the nations of the world. But just as the children of Israel encountered enemy forces that had to be subdued, so do we who are God's children today. God said to Israel, "If you do not drive out the inhabitants of the land, those you allow to remain will become barbs in your eyes and thorns in your sides. They will give you trouble in the land where you will live" (Numbers 33:55).

Our mission as the church, the body of Christ, cannot be accomplished by human "might and power," but only by our Lord's Spirit.

## A personal testimony

Many new missionaries sent from the United States are not aware, at the beginning of their ministries, of their two-fold mission: confronting the spiritual powers of darkness as well as confronting the lost with the gospel. Many who become missionaries have to be shocked into reality—myself among them.

My seminary training had convinced me that to bring people to salvation we needed only to give them the Word of God. Though my seminary training was excellent in offering a superb Bible education, preparation for spiritual conflict was not a part of the program.

After we arrived in France, several years passed during which my wife and I engaged in pretty intense evangelism of a traditional nature, but with little fruit. During those years, however, we became increasingly aware of the spiritual bondage of the people. We realized that, for the most part, their intellectual arguments were simply a smokescreen. Though the French prided themselves as being the most rationalistic people on the globe, evidences of a different kind of spirituality, dark and completely irrational, were everywhere.

After opening our ministry center in the heart of Burgundy, with a far greater focus on prayer and personal relationships, our realization grew that we were not simply confronting the hardness of people's hearts, but spiritual opposition. We tried to list our Bible center in the yellow pages but were told that we did not fit any of their categories. However, in those same yellow pages we found three separate listings for occult practitioners. The city of Lyon, a known center of spiritual darkness, was just to the south of us.

It became evident through our contacts with other Christian workers and missionaries that our experiences were far from unique; in fact, they seemed to be typical.

In the spring of 1980 about forty of us working throughout France banded together to seek to rally people to pray for spiritual awakening and deliverance in France. We sent out brochures called "A Plea for Help." The brochure was printed in a number of evangelical periodicals in different countries. Many churches put aside the first Sunday of each month to intercede for France. People responded from different parts of the world. One of our friends identified more than one hundred groups of believers in various countries praying for France's awakening.

Response to those prayers was not long in coming, though it was not what we had expected. During the summer of 1980 three buildings of evangelical churches in the city of Lyon were burned down; the arsonists were never arrested. Two grown children of workers in an evangelical organization in Lyon died under mysterious circumstances, one shot outside her apartment, another dying by suicide. A prominent pastor, known for his effectiveness in evangelism, moved into Lyon to begin his ministry in one of the churches. Many of us saw in this move renewed hope. Within months his health began to deteriorate, and one of the members of his church confessed that she was a part of an occult group that had put a curse on him, and that he would die. Though he was the object of daily prayer, he died before the end of the year, diagnosed with cancer. Was his cancer related to the curse? Only God knows.

During all that time, inscriptions were painted on the buildings and sidewalks of the city with this message: "Gog is coming." No one could determine who was painting them, or what the message represented. They were painted in blue, the color used by royalists, those hoping for a return to France's royalty. Occult tradition pretends that some strains of France's royalty can be traced back to Christ through Mary Magdalene, who is claimed to have arrived on the southern coast of France pregnant with Jesus' child. All this made us wonder if the antichrist was lurking in the shadows, ready to make his appearance.

Those of us living in France at that time were sobered, convinced that the prayers of God's people had touched a sensitive nerve in the unseen world. Unfortunately, however, the volume and intensity of prayer that we experienced in the 1980s was too short-lived, diminishing by the end of the decade. Yet, though France has not experienced the spiritual awakening that hundreds of believers continue to plead for, the last chapter has not been written. We are convinced that their prayers are kept in heavenly vessels waiting to be poured out on the world at God's appointed time (Revelation 5:8, 8:3-5).

France is only a small part of a world in which Satan, its illegitimate god, has succeeded in blinding the minds of unbelievers. Every true believer has been sent into this world as an ambassador for Jesus Christ. Every believer faces spiritual opposition in bringing truth to the people of this world. Every believer must be covered with Christ's authority and filled with the Spirit's power.

As we learned in the beginning of this chapter, it is not by human might, or human power, but by God's Spirit, and it is in the power of His Spirit that we press on in the mission of the church.

## Discussion questions:

What do we mean when we say that the Great Commission is the church's fundamental law of existence?

Explain the interaction of authority and power in effective mission.

What are the two faces of mission and why must confrontation be two-fold for effective ministry?

## Chapter Sixteen

# The
# Defeated
# Prince

*The unfolding drama of redemption reaches its final chapters in the book of Revelation. Here the veil separating us from the unseen world is stripped away. The book of Revelation moves constantly back and forth between the defeat of Satan and the triumph of the Lamb. The defeat of Satan is a drama woven around his expulsion from heaven, the revelation of the antichrist, the rise of the false prophet, Armageddon, the binding of Satan, and his being cast into the lake of fire.*

"I saw Satan fall like lightning from heaven." Jesus made this statement, recorded in Luke 10:18, to the seventy-two disciples who had been sent out two by two to announce the kingdom. They had returned to their master with joy, saying, "Lord, even the demons submit to us in your name" (Luke 10:17).

Whether these words of Jesus refer to Satan's original fall, or whether our Lord was speaking prophetically, the ability of the disciples to cast out demons was a foretaste of the ultimate downfall of this utterly wicked enemy of God.

Throughout this book we have seen that Satan was stripped of his *authority* through the cross and the resurrection, but that he continues to exercise his *power*. When we open the final book of the

Bible, everything changes. Here we learn how, step by step, Satan and his angels will be stripped of their *power* through incredible manifestations of God's might.

> *The expulsion of Satan is one of the significant events marking the beginning of the great tribulation*

The book of Revelation is the great drama of the end times. It is the final chapter in God's plan of redemption, in which the visible and the invisible dimensions of God's creation intermingle, and we are stunningly confronted with the extraordinary activity of angelic beings. In this chapter we will limit our comments to six great episodes in Satan's final destruction—the war in heaven, the rise of the man of sin, the appearance of the false prophet, Armageddon, the binding of Satan in the abyss, and the casting of Satan into the lake of fire.

### War in heaven

First, the war in heaven. This war is depicted in Revelation 12:7-9.

> And there was war in heaven. Michael and his angels fought against the dragon, and the dragon and his angels fought back. But he was not strong enough, and they lost their place in heaven. The great dragon was hurled down—that ancient serpent called the devil, or Satan, who leads the whole world astray. He was hurled to the earth, and his angels with him.

The text leaves no doubt concerning the identity of the dragon—he is the devil, or Satan. The book of Revelation presents three series of terrible judgments upon the earth, set in the context of seven seals, seven trumpets, and seven bowls. These judgments take place during a seven-year period corresponding with the seventieth week of the prophecy given to Daniel (Daniel 9:25-27). Midway through this seven-year period a number of dramatic events occur, marking the beginning of what is called the period of *great* tribulation, a period lasting three-and-a-half years. The text is precise about the length of this period, for it is referred to as 42 months (Revelation 11:2, 13:5) or 1,260 days (Revelation 11:3, 12:6), corresponding to the "time, times, and half a time" recorded in the prophecy of Daniel (Daniel 7:25, 12:7).

The war in heaven and the expulsion of Satan are the most significant events marking the beginning of this *great* tribulation. Michael, the great archangel, musters his angels in this cosmic conflict against Satan, the "ruler of the kingdom of the air" (Ephesians 2:2). Michael and his angels prevail, armed with the blood of the lamb and the testimony of the saints. Satan and his angels are cast down to the earth.

Immediately after the battle a loud voice from heaven announces the kingdom of God and authority of Christ, for the accuser of the brethren has been hurled down (Revelation 12:10-11). Woe is proclaimed to the earth for the devil is filled with fury, knowing that his time is short (Revelation 12:12).

Try to imagine what it will mean for Satan and his angels to be hurled to the earth. No longer will they have the freedom to move freely in the "heavens," or the world of spirits. They will now be forced to be embodied in living beings, producing hundreds of thousands of the same kind of victims as the man from the region of the Gerasenes who went about naked and violent, possessed by a legion of impure spirits (Mark 5:1-13).

In light of this account of Satan's expulsion from the heavens, one of the most horribly sobering passages of Revelation is in chapter 9. When the fifth angel sounds his trumpet, a star falls from heaven (v. 1). This star is not a meteor; it is an angelic being. The star doubtless refers to Satan himself, especially its identification with "the angel of the Abyss, whose name in Hebrew is Abaddon, and in Greek, Apollyon," which means Destroyer (Revelation 9:11). This angelic being is given the key to the abyss, releasing upon the inhabitants of the earth the multitude of evil spirits imprisoned in that woeful place.

Thus the inhabitants of the earth will be attacked from both above and below—from the demonic spirits cast out of heaven and from those released from their prison under the earth. The agony that these impure spirits will inflict upon those who do not have the seal of God on their forehead is unspeakable. "During those days men will seek death, but will not find it; they will long to die, but death will elude them" (Revelation 9:6).

Praise will break out from the angels in heavenly places, now purified of evil. But intense suffering will fall on the earth (Revelation 12:12).

### The man of sin

Immediately after Satan's expulsion from the heavens, a beast will rise from the sea. Comparing chapter 12 with Revelation 17:15, we can conclude that the sea symbolizes the peoples of the earth, out of which a powerful political dictator will arise. The beast is the man of sin, or the antichrist (1 John 2:18).

> *The antichrist will be a man of exceptional talent who will succeed in gaining great power*

The antichrist will be a man of exceptional talent who will succeed in gaining great power. According to Revelation 13:7-8, the antichrist will be given "power to make war against the saints and to conquer them," as well as to impose "authority over every tribe, people, language, and nation." He will even be the object of worship by those "whose names have not been written in the book of life." Many think that he will arise from a revived Roman empire because of the references in Daniel's prophecy to the fourth world power, which was Rome. Daniel 9:27 indicates that he will make a seven-year "covenant" with God's people, the Jews. However, he will break the covenant in the middle of the seven years, putting an end to their sacrifices and offerings, which will have only recently been reinstated.

We are first introduced to the antichrist in the prophecy of Daniel. In chapter 7 we have the account of the prophet's dream of four beasts. The similarities between Daniel's prophecy and the description in Revelation are striking. The fourth beast represents a great kingdom which will "devour the whole earth" (Daniel 7:23). It has ten horns, representing ten kings. From those ten kings another king will arise, identified in verse 8 as a "little horn," a powerful king who will wage war against the saints and defeat them until the coming of the Ancient of Days (vv. 21-22). He will rule for "a time, times, and half a time" (three and a half years).

In Daniel 8:23-25 he is called "a stern-faced king, a master of intrigue." He will "become very strong, *but not by his own power.*" He will cause devastation, destroying mighty men and holy people and taking his stand even against the Prince of princes. "He will be destroyed, but not by human power." The prophet Daniel again refers to him in 9:26-27, where he is said to set up an "abomination that causes desolation."

Jesus refers to the antichrist—and to this passage in Daniel—in Matthew 24:15-21, where He states that the appearance of the antichrist will mark the beginning of "great distress, unequaled from the beginning of the world until now—and never to be equaled again." The apostle Paul refers to him in 2 Thessalonians 2:3-4, where he says that the day of the Lord will not come "until the rebellion occurs and the man of lawlessness is revealed, the man doomed to destruction. He will oppose and will exalt himself over everything that is called God or is worshiped, so that he sets himself up in God's temple, proclaiming himself to be God."

We are not left to guess why this powerful political figure suddenly becomes unspeakably evil, assuming authority, exacting worship, blaspheming God, and making war against the saints. It is because "the dragon gave the beast his *power* and his *throne* and great *authority*" (Revelation 13:2, emphasis added).

When Satan and his angels are cast from heaven, hundreds of thousands of earth's inhabitants will be "demonized" with impure spirits. But only one inhabitant of the earth will be "Satanized." This man, the antichrist, will become the man of sin, the archenemy of God, the instrument through which Satan will pour out his fury. There is only one other case in recorded history in which Satan himself possessed a human being. His name was Judas (Luke 22:3).

## The false prophet

The antichrist will be a political leader, but he will immediately be joined by another beast, this one coming out of the earth. John's description in Revelation brings us to the immediate conclusion that the second beast is a *religious* leader, identified as the false prophet in Revelation 16:13, 19:20, and 20:10.

The description of the false prophet in Revelation 13:11-18 is vivid. He will "exercise all the authority of the first beast on his behalf." He will make "the earth and its inhabitants worship the first beast." He will perform "great and miraculous signs, even causing fire to come down from heaven to earth in full view of men." He will deceive "the inhabitants of the earth" and will order "them to set up an image in honor of the beast." He will even be "given power to give breath to the image of the first beast," causing it to speak. He will "cause all who refuse to worship the image to be killed."

> *The second beast will be a religious leader, identified as the false prophet*

This beast, whose mysterious number is 666, will be able to control the world's economy by forcing everyone, "small and great, rich and poor, free and slave, to receive a mark on his right hand or on his forehead, so that no one could buy or sell unless he had the mark, which is the name of the beast or the number of his name" (Revelation 13:16-17).

Throughout history it has been evident that political power can usually succeed only when combined with religion. The most powerful movements of history have nearly always been motivated by religious fanaticism. No political ruler will ultimately succeed in totally suppressing the people unless he becomes the object of worship or forms an alliance with religion. The false prophet will succeed in bringing together the peoples of the earth into a global religion, worshiping the antichrist and mercilessly opposing the true saints of God.

## Armageddon

The agony inflicted upon the earth during the time of great tribulation, both by the powers of evil and the judgments of God, will be intense beyond imagination. But it will be brief.

During this period of extreme suffering, seven angels will pour out their bowls of God's wrath upon the inhabitants of the earth given over to the worship of the beast. When the sixth angel pours out his bowl, three evil spirits, resembling frogs, will come out of the mouths of the dragon, the antichrist, and the false prophet. Performing miraculous signs, these spirits go out to the kings of the whole world, gathering them to a place called Armageddon, anticipating the coming of the Lord for the battle on the great day of God Almighty (Revelation 16:12-14).

Armageddon, the Mount of Megiddo, is located in the Plain of Esdraelon, the great battlefield in Israel. Whether Revelation uses the term Armageddon literally or symbolically is of little importance. The text makes it clear that there will be a literal war. At the appointed time, when the kings of the earth are gathered together, the heavens will open and a white horse will appear whose rider is called Faithful and True (Revelation 19:4).

The armies of heaven will follow Him, and out of His mouth will come a sharp sword with which He will strike down the nations. On His thigh will be written this inscription: KING OF KINGS AND LORD OF LORDS. The beast and the kings of the earth and their armies will gather together to make war. They will be defeated. The beast and the false prophet will be captured and thrown alive into the lake of fire (Revelation 19:19-21). The lake of fire is the entrance to eternal hell. Before the spirit departs into outer darkness, the body is consumed. This is the second death.

This is the first recorded instance of any beings being consigned to this terrible place, a place prepared for the devil and his angels (Matthew 25:41).

Then, according to the apostle John's words in Revelation 20:1-3,

> I saw an angel coming down out of heaven, having the key to the Abyss and holding in his hand a great chain. He seized the dragon, that ancient serpent, who is the devil, or Satan, and bound him for a thousand years. He threw him into the Abyss, and locked and sealed it over him, to keep him from deceiving the nations anymore until the thousand years were ended.

## The lake of fire

After telling us that Satan will be bound during the thousand years of Christ's rule over the earth, the apostle John inserts a perplexing phrase that puzzles many readers. He tells us that after the thousand-year reign of Christ, the millennium, Satan "*must* be set free for a short time" (Revelation 20:3, emphasis added). Incredibly, Satan's deceits do not come to their final end with his imprisonment in the abyss. At the end of the millennium "Satan will be released from his prison and will go out to deceive the nations of the four corners of the earth—'Gog and Magog'—to gather them" together for the earth's final battle. A vast army, numerous as sand on the shore, will surround the camp of God's people, the city He loves." Fire will come down from heaven and devour those forces (Revelation 20:7-9).

> *Scripture leaves no doubt about the final destiny of God's archenemy*

After that the devil, who again deceives the nations, will be thrown into the lake of burning sulfur, where the beast and the false prophet will have already been thrown. They will be tormented day and night forever (Revelation 20:10).

Scripture leaves no doubt about the final destiny of God's arch-enemy, the world's second prince. He will never again be released to deceive the nations of the world. But the question that haunts us is why he was allowed the freedom to once again deceive the nations after being defeated at the battle of Armageddon. For a thousand years the world will know peace and prosperity under the rule of its rightful prince, the Lord Jesus Christ. Why then will Satan again be freed to bring to an end this period of peace?

As we ponder this question, we remember all the other questions that have flooded our minds as we have pursued this drama. Why did an omniscient God create a being He knew would become His archenemy? Why did He appoint him the guardian angel of man, His highest creation? Why was he allowed to wreak havoc upon the inhabitants of the earth for centuries? Why was he given the freedom to tempt his Creator? Why was he allowed to orchestrate the Lord's brutal death? Why, though stripped of his authority, has he been able to continue to exert incredible opposition against the church, the object of the Lord's affection?

The drama of redemption occupies a huge period of time, stretching from the fall of Adam to the consignment of Satan to the lake of fire. Why is this period so long? Why has Satan been given such a long leash, allowing him to continue to afflict untold misery upon the inhabitants of this earth?

These questions go to the heart of mankind's most profound mystery—why an all-knowing and all-powerful God permits evil. No amount of human reasoning will give us answers that completely satisfy. But in our attempt to penetrate this mystery, sooner or later we will be confronted by a stark truth: *Satan unwittingly has been the instrument for the demonstration of God's redeeming love.*

Meditate on these simple but profound realities.

Only because mankind fell into Satan's bondage was it pos-sible for God to show the infinite depth of His love.

Only those who have been set free from bondage can experience the love of God in all its fullness.

Only those who experience the love of God in all its fullness can, in return, love God with all their heart, mind, and soul.

Mystery of mysteries: without Satan, mankind would never have known the depth of God's love. Does that mean that God carries the responsibility for Satan's rebellion and Adam's sin? Of course not! Freedom of choice is not an illusion; humans are not puppets. Though the drama of redemption is still veiled in mystery, we can, with the apostle Paul, make this affirmation:

> Oh, the depth of the riches of the wisdom and knowledge of God! How unsearchable his judgments, and his paths beyond tracing out! Who has known the mind of the Lord? Or who has been his counselor? Who has ever given to God, that God should repay him? For from him and through him and to him are all things. To him be the glory forever! Amen (Romans 11:33-36).

## Discussion questions:

How is the rise of the antichrist related to Satan's being cast out of heaven?

Why will the antichrist and the false prophet be able to exercise such extensive power over the earth's inhabitants?

How can we say that without Satan, mankind would have never known the depth of God's love?

# Chapter Seventeen

# The Eternal Prince

*At the appointed time, the King of kings will return to the earth, accompanied by the spirits of those who have already been taken to paradise. He will raise their bodies, transform the living who are redeemed, judge His people, and celebrate His eternal marriage with the church. This will also be a time of unthinkable suffering on the earth. Jesus will then return in power to establish His earthly kingdom of 1,000 years.*

THE FOCUS OF THE PRECEDING CHAPTER WAS SATAN. WE traced the events leading to the final doom of this archenemy of God and mankind. In this chapter our focus will be the triumph of the legitimate and eternal Prince of the earth, the Lord Jesus Christ. God the Son became the last Adam to gain back everything that the first Adam had lost. We will again refer to some of the events covered in chapter 16, but our focus will no longer be on Satan. It will be on our Lord Jesus Christ.

From the moment of His resurrection and exaltation, the Lord Jesus Christ has been the legitimate ruler of the earth. He is the third and final Prince. Paul writes in Philippians 2:9-11, "God exalted him to the highest place and gave him the name that is above every name, that at the name of Jesus every knee should bow, in heaven and on earth and under the earth, and every tongue confess that Jesus Christ is Lord, to the glory of God the Father."

But though our legitimate Prince is seated in *authority* upon His heavenly throne at the right hand of God the Father, He is not yet exercising His *power* directly upon His earthly kingdom. We are living in a period of transition, and the transition has been long.

> *Our Lord Jesus, the rightful prince, will one day return to this earth*

The last recorded question of the disciples to the Lord was, "Lord, are you at this time going to restore the kingdom to Israel?" (Acts 1:6). This question continues to burn in the hearts of the Lord's followers as they echo the cry of Revelation 6:10: "How long, Sovereign Lord, holy and true, until you judge the inhabitants of the earth?" When will our Lord return in His glory to exercise His power?

As we have seen previously, the Lord's answer to us today is the same as His answer to His disciples:

> It is not for you to know the times or dates the Father has set by His own authority. But you will receive power when the Holy Spirit comes on you; *and you will be my witnesses* in Jerusalem, and in all Judea and Samaria, and to the ends of the earth (Acts 1:7-8, emphasis added).

While not losing sight of the blessed hope of Christ's return, our focus is to be upon our earthly mission. Like the disciples who witnessed Jesus' ascension, we are not to spend our lives gazing into the heavens. We have a task to fulfill.

In the midst of the challenges of this mission, however, we are sustained by the same blessed hope that was given by the angels to the disciples. "This same Jesus, who has been taken from you into heaven, *will come back* in the same way you have seen him go into heaven" (Acts 1:11, emphasis added).

## The coming of the Lamb

Yes, our Lord Jesus, the rightful Prince, will one day return to this earth. No other event is more vividly portrayed in the Scriptures. His coming will be in two phases. He will first come as the Lamb who was slain, to unite Himself to His eternal bride. We call this coming "the Rapture." It is significant that in the book of Revelation our Lord is called the Lamb thirty times, in contrast to being called the King only three times. Does that diminish His role as King of kings? Absolutely not! But for all eternity we will be reminded that in order to rule as Prince, Jesus had to be slain as the sacrificial Lamb.

At God's appointed time a trumpet will sound and the saints, dead and alive, will hear the mighty voice of the archangel. Jesus will return "in a flash, in the twinkling of an eye, at the last trumpet. For the trumpet will sound, the dead will be raised imperishable, and we will be changed" (1 Corinthians 15:52). He will be accompanied by the spirits of the saints who have already died; their bodies will be called from the graves and reunited with their spirits. Those saints who are alive will be transformed, and all will be united with the Lord in the air, to be with Him forever (1 Thessalonians 4:13-17).

The preparation of the bride will reach its culmination after all the saints will have appeared before the judgment seat of Christ. "We must all appear before the judgment seat of Christ, that each one may receive what is due him for the things done while in the body, whether good or bad" (2 Corinthians 5:10). We do not know whether all the saints will appear before the judgment seat at the same time, or whether we will appear individually, either at the time we meet our Lord at death, or when He returns at the Rapture.

Once the saints are judged, however, the sound of a great multitude of angels will ring out. John compares this sound to the roar of rushing waters and loud peals of thunder. This multitude of voices will cry out,

> Hallelujah! For our Lord God Almighty reigns. Let us rejoice and be glad and give him glory! For the wedding of the Lamb has come, and his bride has made herself ready. Fine linen, bright and clean, was given her to wear (Revelation 19:6-8).

A mighty angel will proclaim, "Blessed are those who are invited to the wedding supper of the Lamb! ... These are the true words of God" (Revelation 19:9).

Few festivals bring more joy than a wedding feast. The greatest wedding feast of all eternity is yet to come. As we saw in the beginning of this story, the vast multitude of angels shouted for joy when they witnessed the creation of the earth. Those shouts of joy might seem almost insignificant when compared to their ecstasy in witnessing the supreme festival of all time, "the wedding supper of the Lamb."

## The coming of the King

After the wedding feast, at God's appointed time, the heavens will open, revealing a white horse, whose rider is called Faithful and True. The apostle John's description of this rider, in Revelation 19:11-16, is striking: "His eyes are like blazing fire, and on his head are many crowns. ... [His] robe [is] dipped in blood and his name is the Word of God. ... Out of his mouth comes a sharp sword with which to strike down the nations."

The rider is the King of kings and the Lord of lords. He will return to the earth followed by the armies of heaven, composed both of men and angels. As we saw in chapter 16, the coming of the Lord in power and glory will result in the greatest single conflict the earth has ever known, the battle of Armageddon. But the battle will be of short duration. As we saw in the preceding chapter, the antichrist and the false prophet will be captured and thrown alive into the lake of fire. Satan will be confined to the abyss for a thousand years.

> The greatest wedding feast of all eternity is yet to come

Then thrones will be established, and those appointed by the Lord will be seated upon them, including the martyrs of the great tribulation who had refused the mark of the beast on their hands or foreheads. They will rule with Christ upon the earth for a thousand years.

This kingdom of a thousand years, the millennial kingdom, will be the fulfillment of the kingdom promises given to the Jewish nation. Our Lord Jesus Christ is the descendant of David who will sit on the throne of the Holy City. The earth will know a period of great peace and prosperity. Isaiah's prophecies are explicit:

> He will judge between the nations and will settle disputes for many peoples. They will beat their swords into plowshares and their spears into pruning hooks. Nation will not take up sword against nation, nor will they train for war anymore (Isaiah 2:4).

> Of the increase of his government and peace there will be no end. He will reign on David's throne and over his kingdom, establishing and upholding it with justice and righteousness from that time on and forever (Isaiah 9:7).

> *The millennial kingdom will be the fulfillment of the kingdom promises made to Israel*

The wolf will live with the lamb, the leopard will lie down with the goat, the calf and the lion and the yearling together; and a little child will lead them. The cow will feed with the bear, their young will lie down together, and the lion will eat straw like the ox. The infant will play near the hole of the cobra, and the young child put his hand into the viper's nest. They will neither harm nor destroy on all my holy mountain, for the earth will be full of the knowledge of the LORD as the waters cover the sea (Isaiah 11:6-9).

## The final judgment

As we saw in chapter 16, the earth will know another great conflict at the end of the thousand years. Satan will be released from his prison and will go out to deceive the nations in the four corners of the earth and gather them for battle (Revelation 20:7-8). *This battle will be the last time in history that all three of the world's princes will be present at the same time—Adam, Satan, and Christ.* Will there be personal encounter among the three? No one can know. But if so, it will quickly come to an end.

Most people would think that this glorious kingdom should go on forever. Why is it limited to a period of one thousand years? Perhaps the best answer is that the release of Satan is necessary to reveal the true nature of men's hearts. During the thousand years the inhabitants of the earth will be compelled to submit to Christ. *To enter the new heavens and the new earth, however, they too will have to be redeemed through personal choice.*

> *The final battle will be the last time that all three of the world's princes will be present at the same time*

Jesus is the Lamb not only for those who are redeemed before His coming; He is also the Lamb for those who enter the millennial kingdom or are born during His rule of a thousand years. How their choice will be known is not completely clear. The prophet Ezekiel even speaks of a renewal of the Old Testament sacrificial system (Ezekiel 40-48). Most interpret these sacrifices to be as a memorial to the sacrifice of the Lamb once for all on the cross. Is it possible, however, that the sacrifices will provide one of the means by which faith in the true Lamb will be shown?

The final conflict, after which Satan will be thrown into the lake of fire, will be followed by a huge resurrection. This resurrection, however, will be devoid of hope. Hades will give up its dead. People of all ages whose names are not recorded in the Lamb's book of life—those who have never experienced the cleansing of the blood of the Lamb—will be brought before the

Great White Throne on which the Lord, the great judge, will be seated. Earth and sky will flee from His presence. Books will be opened containing the life stories of the spiritually dead from the beginning of time. They will look in vain for their names in the Lamb's book of life.

Their fate is dreadful beyond comprehension. Those whose names are not in the book of life will be thrown into the lake of fire. This, says the apostle John, is the second death (Revelation 20:11-15).

## Jesus the Lamb, Prince forever

At the end of the millennium, the earth as we know it now will be redeemed. According to the apostle Peter, "The heavens will disappear with a roar; the elements will be destroyed by fire, and the earth and everything in it will be laid bare" (2 Peter 3:10). That indicates that at the end of the millennial kingdom the earth will be devoid of all its human inhabitants. Scripture does not tell us what will happen to the righteous who are still upon the earth at the end of the millennium. Will they experience another rapture? Will their bodies be transformed into spiritual bodies, just as will be true for those living on the earth when the Lord raptures His church? We can only imagine.

One thing is certain, however. There will be a new heaven and a new earth. "The kingdom of this world [will] become the kingdom of our Lord and of his Christ, and he will reign for ever and ever" (Revelation 11:15). When we open our Bibles to Revelation 21 we begin to discover the marvels of this new heaven and new earth, and of the bride, the church, now pictured as a city coming down in all her glory.

## *Discussion questions:*

Explain the difference between our Lord's coming *for* the saints, and His coming *with* His saints.

Since the judgment of the believer occurred at the cross, what is the purpose of the judgment seat of Christ?

If the church is already the bride of Christ, why is the marriage feast yet future?

# Chapter Eighteen

# All
# Things
# New

*At the end of the thousand years, the earth and its heavens will be vacated and totally renovated. The church, the Holy City, will descend from heaven to the earth, where the eternal rule of the Lamb will occur. All that was lost through Adam will be restored, and the third prince, the Lamb of God, will rule forever as the God-man.*

The Bible begins with these words: "In the beginning, God created the heavens and the earth" (Genesis 1:1). When we come to the end of the Bible we read: "Then I saw a *new* heaven and a *new* earth, for the first heaven and the first earth had passed away" (Revelation 21:1, emphasis added). Between those two statements God unveils the supreme drama of redemption with its three princes. It is a drama being played out simultaneously in two dimensions—the visible and the invisible—and it is a drama in which each one of us is playing a role. We are participants, not just spectators, in history's phenomenal story.

When we hear the word "redemption" we often limit our thoughts to the redemption of mankind. There is another aspect of redemption which is less evident to most of us, however. It is the redemption of the entire creation. Few of us realize how closely all creation is bound to mankind. Because Adam was the prince of the earth, all creation died with him when he sinned and suffered death. At that time the heavens and the earth began their long process of disintegration that continues to the present. Full redemption will be complete only when the heavens and earth are made new.

The apostle Paul brings this out vividly in Romans 8:19-22:

> The creation waits in eager expectation for the sons of God to be revealed. For the creation was subjected to frustration, not by its own choice, but by the will of the one who subjected it, in hope that the creation itself will be liberated from its bondage to decay and brought into the glorious freedom of the children of God. We know that the whole creation has been groaning as in the pains of childbirth right up to the present time.

> *Redemption will be complete only when the heavens and earth are made new*

Just as death must inevitably precede resurrection in our lives, it will be necessary that the present earth with its heavens be destroyed so that God might make all things new. After telling us that the heavens will disappear with a roar, that the elements will be destroyed by fire, and that the earth and everything in it will be laid bare, the apostle Peter hastens to assure us that "in keeping with his promise we are looking forward to a *new* heaven and a *new* earth, the home of righteousness" (2 Peter 3:10-13, emphasis added).

Destruction, however, does not mean annihilation. The new earth will not be an entirely new creation; it will be a total restoration and glorification. Our earth will be redeemed.

### John's final vision

The new heaven and earth are the concern of John's final vision in the extraordinary book of Revelation. In contemplating the apostle's words, it is helpful to remember that the term "heaven" has more than one meaning in the Scriptures, as is true of some of the other biblical terms we have examined. For instance, the apostle Paul, in 2 Corinthians 12:2, speaks of being caught up into the *third* heaven, implying, of course, that this heaven is one of three.

Just what are these three heavens?

The first heaven is the one referred to in Genesis 1:1, where we read that God created the heavens and the earth. This refers to the heavens which are visible from the earth. Some would limit it to the earth's atmosphere; others would include the sun, moon, planets, and stars, which seems to be the meaning in Psalm 19:1: "The heavens declare the glory of God; the skies proclaim the work of his hands."

Though the second heaven is more difficult to identify, Scripture makes it pretty clear that it is the abode of the spirit world. In unveiling God's great plan for our age, Ephesians 1:10 talks about bringing "all things in heaven and on earth under one head, even Christ." Just as the earth is the habitation of mankind, the term "heaven" in this passage refers to the domain of angelic beings. We have seen that the second heaven will be purified when Michael and his angels fight against Satan and his forces, prevailing against them and casting them from heaven to the earth (Revelation 12:7-9). In that passage it is evident that the term "heaven" does not refer to the place of God's throne. As a result of the war Satan and his army of evil spirits will no longer have the freedom to roam at will, but will be confined to the earth.

The third heaven is the dwelling place of God, where God has His throne. Paul was caught up into this heaven. The experience was so intense that he was not sure whether he was in or out of the body (2 Corinthians 12:1-4). The same experience was given to the apostle John:

> After this I looked, and there before me was a door standing open in heaven. And the voice I had first heard speaking to me like a trumpet said, 'Come up here, and I will show you what must take place after this.' At once I was in the Spirit, and there before me was a throne in heaven with someone sitting on it (Revelation 4:1-2).

Though Paul was not given permission to share what he saw in the third heaven, such was not the case with John. He was commanded to write, giving us the book of Revelation. He writes in chapter 4 about God on the throne, encircled by a rainbow, surrounded by the twenty-four thrones of the elders. There are flashes of lightning, rumblings and peals of thunder, and blazing lamps, representing the seven spirits of God. Foreboding creatures before the throne cry out day and night, "Holy, holy, holy is the Lord God Almighty, who was, and is, and is to come" (Revelation 4:8). The elders fall down before God laying their crowns at His feet. John saw the Lamb and heard all the creatures surrounding the throne cry out, as they fell before Him, "Worthy is the Lamb, who was slain, to receive power and wealth and wisdom and strength and honor and glory and praise!" (Revelation 5:11).

We have learned in previous chapters that as adopted children of God, we are *already* seated with Christ at the right hand of God in the third heaven with respect to our *legal* status. At death, when "the earthly tent we live in is destroyed" (2 Corinthians 5:1) and we leave this earth, our spirits will be ushered into paradise and the presence of God. Then, at our Lord's appointed time, our spirits will return with Him to be joined to our resurrected body and united to the Lord as His eternal bride. We will reign with Him for a thousand years.

It is at the end of this time that the "first earth" will be vacated for its total renovation.

## The new earth

We can only try to imagine what the new earth will be like. The main challenge of interpreting Revelation is to determine what is symbolic and what is literal. Revelation was given to John in "signs," according to Revelation 1:1, where it says literally, "He sent and *signified* it by his angel to his servant John." *Signified* means "to express by signs."

Yet however we might interpret the details, the text makes it evident that the earth will be a physical earth and that we will have physical bodies, even though they will be resurrected and "spiritual," in the sense that they will be totally under the control of our spirits and capable of living in both worlds—the visible and the invisible.

*New Earth*

The new earth will be the culmination of all the wisdom and beauty of the Creator. In all of our immense universe, the earth is the center of God's attention. Scientists may scoff at such a statement, seeing our planet as only a speck of dust in the immensity of space. Yet you cannot have it any other way if you take God's revelation seriously. That is true whether you consider the earth in its past or future. Look at the evidence. There is but one Son of God—only one. Two thousand years ago He willingly became a member of the *human* race. He was born *on this earth*, and it is here that He died on the cross. When He left this earth, He promised to return—*to this earth*. It is *here* that He will establish His throne and rule. And it is *to this earth* that the new Jerusalem, the eternal Holy City, will descend.

> *The new earth will be the culmination of all the wisdom and beauty of the Creator*

## The Holy City

Yes, though the new earth with its heavens will be glorious beyond comprehension, its splendor will be surpassed by something even more magnificent—"the Holy City, the new Jerusalem, coming down out of heaven from God, prepared as a bride beautifully dressed for her husband" (Revelation 21:2).

The vision of this spectacular bridal procession pushes language to its limit. Even the extravagant symbolism of this amazing passage is woefully inadequate in conveying the magnificence of the Holy City. It shines with the very glory of God. Its brilliance is like a costly jewel, clear as crystal. It is perfect in its proportions. Its foundations are precious gems. Its gates are pearls. Its streets are pure gold.

Just what is the New Jerusalem, the Holy City? *The New Jerusalem*

Traditionally, most people reading these words have simply seen them as a description of heaven itself. Many aspects of the description have become popularized, such as the "pearly gates" and "streets of gold." Some have actually studied the dimensions of the city to attempt to calculate whether it will be large enough to hold the redeemed of all ages, estimating just how much space each one will have!

If we are to take the text seriously, however, we will have to refrain from identifying the Holy City with heaven. This text makes a distinction between three things—heaven, earth, and the Holy City. The Holy City is not heaven, because it comes down *from* heaven. The Holy City is not the redeemed earth, because it is apparent that it comes down *to* the earth.

> *The Holy City is none other than the church, the bride of the Lord Jesus Christ*

The Holy City is clearly identified by one of the seven angels who had the bowls of the seven last plagues to be inflicted on the earth. His words could not be clearer: "Come, I will show you the bride, the wife of the Lamb" (Revelation 21:9).

The Holy City is none other than the church, the bride of the Lord Jesus Christ. This scene is the culmination of Ephesians 5:25-27: "Christ loved the church and gave himself up for her to make her holy, cleansing her by the washing with water through the word, and to present her to himself as a radiant church, without stain or wrinkle or any other blemish, but holy and blameless."

For those who have problems identifying the church with a city, let us not forget that the Bible uses many metaphors to portray the church: a building, a body, a flock, a vine, and a family, to name a few. If we do not have a problem identifying the church as a body, we should not have a problem identifying her as a city. Each metaphor brings out an element of the essence of the church.

The church is the eternal object of Christ's love. He gave Himself for her in His infinite sacrifice. His purpose is to make her holy, cleansing her through His Word. In that fabulous wedding feast He will present her in all her glory to Himself. And now, in this passage, she is displayed in triumphal procession before the watching universe as the glorious church. The description is fabulous. She has incredible beauty and perfection.

The supreme purpose of God in the drama of redemption is the calling out and perfecting of the bride of Christ. Through the church the wall of hostility between Jew and Gentile and the old and the new covenants has been eternally broken down, for on its gates are written the names of the twelve tribes of Israel, and on its foundation are written the names of the twelve apostles of the Lamb.

Yet as we read on, we discover that even the glory of the church pales in comparison with the glory of the *Lord* in Revelation 21:22-23: "I did not see a temple in the city, because the Lord God Almighty and the Lamb are its temple. The city does not need the sun or the moon to shine on it, for the glory of God gives it light, and the Lamb is its lamp." The glories of the eternal church defy our imagination. Yet the focus of our worship will not be the church's glories, but the glories of the one who gives it its brilliant light—the Lord God Almighty, revealing Himself as the Lamb.

The city of God will be free of sorrow. During the few weeks that have preceded the writing of these words I have shed more tears than during the rest of my entire life. God sent His angels to take my adorable wife of 56 years into His presence without warning. There is great joy in knowing that she is with the Lord, but the pain of separation has been intense. Yet in that glorious city God "will wipe away every tear from [our] eyes. There will be no more death or mourning or crying or pain, for the old order of things [will have] passed away" (Revelation 21:4).

The city of God will be free from evil: "Outside are the dogs, those who practice magic arts, the sexually immoral, the murderers, the idolaters, and everyone who loves and practices falsehood" (Revelation 22:15). That anyone would willingly choose outer darkness over the light of God's presence is the mystery of all mysteries.

## A Prince forever

When the seventh angel sounds his trumpet, loud voices will cry out from heaven saying, "The kingdom of the world has become the kingdom of our Lord and of his Christ, and he will reign for ever and ever" (Revelation 11:15). Jesus is the King of kings and the Lord of lords (Revelation 19:16). The first prince, Adam, ruled only a few days. The usurper, Satan, was stripped of all authority. The third Prince, Jesus, is the Prince whose kingdom will never end. His reign will be eternal.

> *Jesus will reign not only as God, but as a man*

Jesus will reign not only as God, but as a man. When God created the earth, He decreed that man would be its ruler. Jesus did not become a man merely for His thirty or so years on the earth. Jesus, though fully God, remains fully man, as we saw in 1 Timothy 2:5, which refers to our Lord as the *man* Jesus Christ. The enormity of this truth completely shatters our imagination. To regain what Adam lost, Jesus had to clothe Himself with humanity. As the seed of the woman, He crushed the head of the serpent. As a man He will reign forever on the throne of His father David, as the Root of Jesse.

Jesus is our Prince forever. We shall forever be filled with awe and wonder as we bow before Him. "Now we see but a poor reflection as in a mirror; then we shall see face to face. Now I know in part; then I shall know fully, even as I am fully known" (1 Corinthians 13:12).

God's revelation ends with an invitation, a promise, and a prayer. It is with these words from Revelation 21:17-20 that we end this book.

The invitation: "Come, take the free gift of the water of life."

The promise: "I am coming soon."

The prayer: "Come, Lord Jesus."

## Discussion questions:

Why do you think the entire creation was subjected to the curse as a result of Adam's sin?

What does the symbolic representation of the church as the New Jerusalem and the Holy City teach us?

On what basis do we say that our Lord will rule forever both as God and man?

# A
# Final
# Word

You have finished the last chapter in the story of the three great princes who have held authority over the earth—Adam, Satan, and Christ. Your journey has led you through the most overwhelming saga of all eternity—the drama of redemption. Hopefully, reflecting more deeply on the truths of God's revelation has had an impact on your life. We pray that you have gained a greater appreciation of the depth of God's wisdom and of His love toward us, demonstrated in our Lord's incredible sacrifice.

Before you close this book, however, I want to ask you a solemn question: Which of these three princes are *you* serving—Adam, Satan, or Christ?

Your first reaction to this question may well be confusion. After all, Adam lived and died at the very dawn of history. Satan is no longer the prince of this world; his legitimacy was stripped away at the cross. And if you consider yourself a believer in Christ, you probably have never called into question your allegiance to Him.

Look again, however, at the question. It is not, "Who *is* your prince?" It is "Which of these three princes are you *serving?*"

## *Serving Adam: devotion to self*

Let's talk again about Adam. He left a legacy to every member of the human race—the sinful nature. In a very real sense, to live according to the sinful nature is to serve Adam, even though thousands of years have passed since he walked on the earth.

Just as Adam put self before God, plunging creation into chaos, we are all daily tempted to make self first. If there is one expression of the sinful nature that seems to rise above all others, it is *devotion to self.* The enticement to self-worship is so powerful that no one has escaped it. For billions of people, God is spelled *e-g-o.*

The values of the secular world system grow out of man's love of self. Throughout history self-love has been perfected to such a degree that in many societies man has been deified. In other societies whole movements have been founded on the glory of man, such as the Enlightenment, the term which gave Paris the designation "city of light." Paris' more recent arch of triumph, dedicated by President Mitterand in 1989 on the Place de la Défense, is termed "a monument to the triumph of humanity."

Probably few of you reading these words would ever think of intentionally glorifying yourself above the Creator. We are, however, living in a world-system based on "the pride of life." Self-gratification is the chief tool of marketing in our consumer society. "What's in it for me?" too easily becomes the first response even of those who claim the Lord as their master.

There is only one cure for self-love. It is *death.* Jesus made it very plain that just as He was nailed to the cross for us, we must take up our cross for Him. To take up the cross means to die to self. Jesus' words are clear: "Whoever finds his life will lose it, and whoever loses his life for my sake will find it" (Matthew 10:39). The apostle Paul echoes this necessity: "I have been crucified with Christ and I no longer live, but Christ lives in me. The life I live in the body, I live by faith in the Son of God, who loved me and gave himself for me" (Galatians 2:20).

We have been rescued from the dominion of darkness in order to be brought into the kingdom of the Son God loves (Colossians 1:13). The kingdom of the Lord is wherever Christ reigns as King. Though we are *in* the world, we must constantly be on guard against being *of* the world. When we are overcome by this world's demands, it is all too easy to become our own little gods, forgetting that we are to seek, first and always, the kingdom of God and His righteousness.

If, while claiming Christ as your Savior, you are still serving self, you are squandering your most precious possession—your life. To live for self is to see much of our life consumed as wood, hay, and stubble, when we stand before the judgment seat of our Lord. To serve the Prince of all princes, our lives are to be daily laid on the altar as a sacrifice to Him.

> Therefore, I urge you, brothers [and sisters], in view of God's mercy, to offer your bodies as living sacrifices, holy and pleasing to God—this is your spiritual act of worship. Do not conform any longer to the pattern of this world, but be transformed by the renewing of your mind. Then you will be able to test and approve what God's will is—His good, pleasing, and perfect will (Romans 12:1-2).

## Serving Satan: bondage

Though stripped of all legitimacy as the prince of this world, Satan is still fanatically grasping for authority over mankind, and tragically he is highly successful for billions of the earth's inhabitants. Paul calls him "the god of this world" and John says, "the whole world is under the control of the evil one" (2 Corinthians 4:4, 1 John 5:19).

We have seen in this book how Satan so skillfully uses the world, the flesh, and occult practices and religions to enslave men and women and to gain their allegiance. Our modern society has greatly added to his arsenal of weapons with the proliferation of mind-altering drugs, unnatural sexual behavior, and New Age forms of spirituality.

You may have kept yourself free of the most blatant tactics that our enemy uses to bring people under his control. There is no doubt, however, that Satan continues to lead thousands of believers into spiritual bondage. He does it by establishing strongholds in our minds.

Are you free from Satan's effort to establish strongholds in your mind and heart? Or are you struggling with obsessive habits and thought patterns that have effectively quenched the Spirit's power in your life? Help will not come through what Paul calls "the weapons of this world"—good intentions, legalistic resolutions, turning over a new leaf, or counseling devoid of a spiritual worldview. Spiritual bondage requires spiritual deliverance. "The weapons we fight with are not the weapons of this world. On the contrary, they have divine power to demolish strongholds" (2 Corinthians 10:4). Every thought must be taken captive and made obedient to Christ, our rightful prince. We must "put aside the deeds of darkness and put on the armor of light" (Romans 13:12).

If you have read carefully the pages of this book and have sought to take its concepts personally, you know that freedom can come only through frank confession of anything that has given Satan a foothold in your life and through affirming your position in Christ. May you begin each day by clothing yourself with God's armor and actively resisting the devil through prayer and the sword of the Spirit, the Word of God.

## Serving Christ: freedom

"It is for freedom that Christ has set us free." With these words Paul begins the fifth chapter of Galatians. We have been called to be free—free from bondage to the world, the flesh, and the devil.

Though it may seem to be a contradiction in terms, freedom comes from *submission*: submission to the Prince of all princes, Jesus Christ. Jesus is the final Prince; there will be no more. His reign will be forever. We have the privilege of being a part of His eternal kingdom. To reign with Him throughout all ages, however, we must joyfully submit to His reign in our lives here and now.

Jesus has given us this incredible privilege. Offering our lives to Him means receiving Him as our Savior, accepting by faith the truth that He perished on the cross because of our sins, and receiving eternal life as a gift of His grace. It means submitting to Him as the Lord of our lives, presenting ourselves fully to Him as a living sacrifice, and allowing Him to use our bodies as His instruments for fulfilling His will. It means choosing every day to walk in the truth of our spiritual identity—what it means to be "in Christ." It means becoming a part of His eternal church and becoming one of His ambassadors, fulfilling our part in God's great plan of bringing together all things, both in heaven and on earth, under the Lord's headship. It means ministering to God by falling down before Him in daily worship.

Has reflecting on the unfolding drama of redemption helped you to enter into a fuller understanding of God's wisdom? Has it confronted your inmost being with the magnitude of the sacrifice of our Lord in eternally becoming a man and undergoing infinite suffering to deliver you from eternal bondage? Have you experienced a fresh vision of the love of your Lord for you personally?

If so, you realize that there is only one response worthy of your consideration. It is to serve our Lord Jesus Christ, the Prince of all princes, with all your mind, heart, and being.

For Christ's love compels us, because we are convinced that one died for all, and therefore all died. And he died for all, that those who live should no longer live for themselves, but for him who died for them and was raised again (2 Corinthians 5:14-15).

# Scripture
# Index